The
SURPASSING!
Life

52
Practical Ways
to Achieve
Personal Excellence

BRAD REX

May you always have a
Surpassing! life.

Brad Rex

June, 2012

Visit us on-line at:

www.thesurpassinglife.com
www.bradrex.com

Printed in the United States of America

First Printing: 2012

Library of Congress Control Number: 2012908191
ISBN 978-0-9855519-0-2 (print version)
ISBN 978-0-9855519-1-9 (ebook version)

*To my beautiful wife, Nancy, who has taught
me an incredible life lesson of love*

*To James, Monica, and Natalie for the
blessing of being your Dad*

To God—thank you

It is necessary to try to surpass oneself always;
this occupation ought to last as long as life.
— QUEEN CHRISTINA OF SWEDEN
(1626–1689)

Table of Contents

Why Live a Surpassing Life?

ARE YOU HAPPY? Are you overperforming in your life and leadership? If you were to get graded right now, would you get an A+? Are you using your talents fully, developing strong relationships, feeling better and stronger every day, increasing your financial resources, known for a great reputation, leading your people well, successful and knowledgeable? If so, congratulations! There is no need for you to read this book.

But, if you feel you still have opportunity in your life, that you have more to give and receive, that you are not living a life beyond measure, that you would like to increase your happiness and satisfaction, I would like to welcome you to the Surpassing Life. Surpass means to "exceed expectations" and do more than you thought possible.

In *The Surpassing! Life*, I will share with you fifty-two life lessons to help you achieve personal excellence. During my "eclectic" life, I've had the benefit of many different roles, including:

- Nuclear submarine officer
- Strategic planner for British Petroleum and Disney
- Oil futures and options trading group manager during the first Gulf War
- Plastic resin salesman
- Finance Leader for Walt Disney Parks and Resorts, including the team that negotiated Hong Kong Disneyland
- Leader of Disney's Epcot theme park after 9/11

- ▶ Chief Customer Officer for Hilton Grand Vacations
- ▶ Entrepreneur
- ▶ Consultant
- ▶ Public speaker
- ▶ Author
- ▶ Church starter and elder
- ▶ Husband for over thirty years
- ▶ Father of a son and twin daughters

I've attended incredible schools, including the United States Naval Academy and Harvard Business School. I've met fascinating people and traveled around the world. My mentors have been world-class leaders with invaluable lessons. Through all this, I have been blessed with great knowledge that can benefit you in your life.

These lessons can dramatically improve your life and leadership. By applying the information in this book, you can increase your happiness, improve your health, have more money, develop strong new relationships, become more knowledgeable, release your leadership potential, and succeed. Come join me, and surpass your wildest dreams!

How to Use This Book

*T*HE *SURPASSING! LIFE* has fifty-two short sections with ideas to dramatically improve your life and leadership. You can read through from start to finish, read individual chapters or focus on single ideas. Some people read one idea per week, to have a year of surpassing thinking.

Regardless of the path you choose, don't attempt to do everything at once. Pick a few items and do them for twenty-eight days. After doing something daily for twenty-eight days, scientists have found that your brain actually changes and you create a habit. Notice how your life is better, which will reinforce the habit. Then, select a few more items and do them for twenty-eight days. Before you know it, you will have made significant improvements in your life, and be on your way to excelling beyond measure!

CHAPTER 1

Money Beyond Measure

---

*He that is of the opinion money will do everything may
well be suspected of doing everything for money.*
— BENJAMIN FRANKLIN

*All the perplexities, confusions, and distress in America arise,
not from defects in their constitution or confederation, not
from want of honor or virtue, so much as from the downright
ignorance of the nature of coin, credit, and circulation.*
— JOHN ADAMS

Money is better than poverty, if only for financial reasons.
— WOODY ALLEN

*Dishonest money dwindles away, but whoever
gathers money little by little makes it grow.*
— BIBLE, PROVERBS 13:11

B ESIDES GOOD HEALTH, having adequate financial resources
is foundational to enjoying an excellent life. Constantly
worrying about money or bill collectors will drain your energy
and constrain growth. Most people make a number of mistakes
when managing their careers and money that cost them dearly.
By implementing the ideas in this chapter, you can achieve
financial freedom.

5

1. A $23 Cup of Coffee

If you would be wealthy, think of saving as well as getting.
— BENJAMIN FRANKLIN

Forbes has come out with its list of the richest people in America. One of them is the CEO of Starbucks. His secret is that he doesn't buy coffee at Starbucks.
— CONAN O'BRIEN

Twenty-three dollars for a cup of coffee. Most people would say this is a ludicrous price to pay for a jolt of java. Yet millions of people spend $4 for a Starbucks daily. What they don't realize is that if they saved that $4 and invested it for thirty years at 6 percent interest, they would receive $23. The compounding effect of money multiplies the benefit of saving a dollar today, for much greater return in the future.

Companies spend billions of dollars in marketing and advertising to create dissatisfaction and fear, and cause you to spend your money, often on unnecessary things. As an example, take bottled water. The United States has the safest public water system in the world. Yet, we also have the largest bottled water sales. In 1976, the average American consumed a gallon and a half of bottled water each year. By 2008, the number had grown to about thirty gallons of bottled water per person in the US.[1] This equates to 320 twelve-ounce plastic bottles. At $1 apiece, the average spending of $320 a year on water would be

---

[1] Per Peter Gleick, author of *Bottled and Sold: The Story Behind Our Obsession with Bottled Water*

worth over $1,800 in thirty years, just for not drinking bottled water for one year. If you cut out bottled water for thirty years and saved the difference, it would equal $27,000! By using a refillable water bottle and filling it from the tap, you can add $27,000 to your retirement account.

Ongoing expenses provide the greatest opportunity for reduction and savings. A few years ago, I calculated how much I was spending for various types of insurance—car, home, life, health—and was astounded at the result. I had stayed with the same company for my car and homeowners insurance for thirty years, without comparing rates. With teenage drivers and living in hurricane-prone Florida, my costs were exorbitant. By shopping around, I reduced my auto insurance by 50 percent. I then found out that I could cut my homeowners insurance by the same amount by having an inspection and removing unnecessary coverage. New term life insurance gave me more protection at lower cost. And, by switching to high-deductible health insurance and dropping my vision and dental plans, I lowered my costs and saved on taxes. The net effect was savings of over $10,000 per year, equating to over $700,000 for my retirement account in thirty years. While I'm thrilled with this result, I am also chagrined to think about overpaying for all those years, and my lost savings that benefited the insurance companies. Learn from my mistake and do an annual review of all of your insurance, comparison shop your rates, take the minimal coverage and save the difference.

Similarly, you should review all your monthly expenses at least once a year. Do you really watch all those premium cable channels? If you call your cell phone company, will they give you a better rate? Did you sign up for recurring services that you no longer use, like computer service agreements or online games? You may be surprised at how much you can save, and remember that for every dollar you save this year and for the next thirty, you will be adding $73 to your retirement account. That is a surpassing return!

Action Points

- Recognize the compounding value of money and the benefit of savings in creating great wealth.
- Make your own coffee and bank the savings.
- Don't buy bottled water.
- Shop for cheaper insurance and reduce your coverage.
- Review and reduce all your monthly expenses.

Payoff

Financial freedom, and hundreds of thousands of dollars in your retirement account!

2. Satisfying Returns

Never invest your money in anything
that eats or needs repairing.
— BILLY ROSE

I'm a Harvard MBA, so you would think that I know how to invest money. However, over the years, my education has outsmarted me. I've invested in all kinds of instruments and funds, including stocks, bonds, options, real estate, venture capital, private equity, commodities, REITS and partnerships. I've paid significant fees for financial advisors, money managers, accountants, general partners, commissions and lawyers. I've made money and lost money, crowing about wins and then lamenting (and trying to forget) losses. And, as I look back, I realize that I could have made much more money and had a much easier life as an individual investor if I had just invested simply.

In an excellent article in the *Wall Street Journal* entitled "A Simple Recipe for Investors: Less Can Often Lead to More,"[2] Jonathan Burton describes how a simple portfolio of a US stock fund, an international stock fund and a bond fund in a 35/15/50 percent ratio has delivered a very satisfying 9.1 percent annual return over the last twenty-five years.[3] Using low cost

---

[2] "A Simple Recipe for Investors: Less Can Often Lead to More," Jonathan Burton, *Wall Street Journal*, September 2, 2010. Instead of a bond fund, you can also use laddered bonds to ensure a return of principal at maturity.

[3] Recall that the savings growth section used a 6 percent annual return. Nine percent would boost those returns substantially. For example, $1 invested at 9 percent for thirty years would be worth over $13, compared to $5.75 at a 6 percent return.

mutual funds from Vanguard or Fidelity, you can set up this simple investment plan for both your savings and retirement accounts. You can make monthly savings contributions and automatically split the contribution to go into each fund in the correct percentage. Once a year, you "rebalance" the account to maintain the same 35/15/50 percent ratio by selling funds that are over the ratio and buying the funds that are below it.

A major benefit of this simple technique is that you are not subject to market emotion or the "investment product of the week." You won't get swept up in dot.com mania, mortgage backed bonds, hot stock tips, gold, oil, hedge funds or whatever your broker is pushing that month. Even in a severe downturn, this portfolio will lose much less than more aggressive approaches, and you will not cash out at a low point based on fear. The rebalancing discipline ensures you sell at higher points and buy at lower prices for each asset class.

This portfolio is tax- and fee-efficient. By only trading once a year, you minimize your taxable gains and commissions. With low cost funds, more of your money goes into investing rather than fees. Because it is so simple, you can do it yourself, saving the cost (and pressure) of a financial advisor and, without any complicated investments, you won't need an accountant to help you do your taxes.

Some people may still have a burning desire to "play the market." If you fit that description, then put 90 percent of your money into the simple portfolio and use the other 10 percent to invest in whatever you desire. This lets you play, while still protecting the bulk of your savings. You also can objectively compare your performance to the passive portfolio. My bet is that you will find the simple portfolio provides the better return over time.

Action Points

- Simplify your portfolio with a 35 percent US stock fund, 15 percent international stock fund and 50 percent bond fund split.
- Rebalance annually.

 ## Payoff

A worry-free, tax- and fee-efficient investment program with solid returns.

3. Rich Rewards

It is possible to give freely and become more wealthy,
but those who are stingy will lose everything. The
generous prosper and are satisfied; those who
refresh others will themselves be refreshed.
— BIBLE, PROVERBS 11:24–25

A good exercise for the heart is to bend
down and help another up.
— ANONYMOUS

My wife and I have been able to give a substantial amount of money away during the past ten years. We did not set this as a target or have any type of long-range plan. We got involved in our church and community, and met needs as they arose. Our only regret is that we did not give away more, as we believe our lives have been richly rewarded as we have shared our time, talents and money with others.

When you give money away, you prove that money does not control you. We all know people whose lives and emotions are centered on money—acquiring it, investing it, spending it and manipulating others with it. When they get more money, they are happy. When they lose money, they are depressed. Their emotions follow the stock market, and they are paranoid about protecting each dollar. They are also never satisfied with the amount of money they have. When John D. Rockefeller, the richest man in the world at the time, was asked, "How much money is enough?" he replied, "Just one dollar more." Later in life, Rockefeller became generous and spent his remaining years as a philanthropist. Those who knew him said that he found a peace in those years that had eluded him for most of his life.

Some people, particularly televangelists, proclaim the "prosperity gospel" of giving away money to get more money back. Of course, these prophets tell you to give them your money, which makes them the ones who prosper. There have certainly been cases where someone who gives away money is rewarded with more money. But, more frequently, those who are generous receive much greater gifts of relationships, peace, security, freedom, respect and learning. Over the years, I have been amazed, as gifts we have given anonymously to individuals have been "returned" with interest. For example, we met a financial need anonymously for a couple in our church. The husband was a great youth sports coach and the next season he "just happened" to pick one of our children for his team. Would that have happened anyway if we had not been generous? It is certainly possible, but a number of similar experiences over the years have convinced me that situations like these are not coincidences for generous people.

There are smart and foolish ways to give away money. I encourage radical, *rational* generosity. Here are a few thoughts, many learned from my mistakes:

- Budget your giving. When you budget your giving, you ensure that you are not giving "leftovers" (which often means zero) and you are also not being too extravagant and thus creating future regrets. Many recommend 10 percent of your income for donations, and this is a good place to start. The benefit of doing a percentage is that the absolute amount grows automatically as your income increases. Once you get to a level of income that meets your needs, you should consider increasing the percentage. If you receive an unexpected payment, like a large bonus, you may want to give a higher percentage. My wife and I always looked at bonuses as just that—a "bonus." We used bonus money to increase our giving and savings, and spent 10 to 20 percent for one-time items, but we never increased our lifestyle to match expected bonus amounts. This way, we never counted on bonuses, and weren't impacted if they were reduced or went away.

► Don't give emotionally. Amazingly, over two-thirds of donors don't do any research before donating money to an organization. My worst giving decisions have been when I heard or read an emotional appeal and then gave money, only to find out later that the organization was not efficient or spent most its income on fundraising rather than helping others. You should never feel coerced into giving, or give out of a sense of obligation rather than willingness. Research an organization by going to a website such as www.charitynavigator.com. You would do the same for any other "purchase," so why not do your homework when contributing money?

► Demand the highest level of financial accountability. Idealistic, visionary leaders start many non-profit organizations. These leaders provide compelling visions for their organizations that motivate people to join and donate. However, the administrative and managerial skills of these leaders are often weak. Money is not properly accounted for and can be wasted through a lack of fiscal discipline. The leader is not dishonest (usually), just not knowledgeable or careful when it comes to money. The worst situation is when a non-profit goes bankrupt, and the donors see their dreams about how the money will help others evaporate. To prevent this, you should ensure that your donations only go to non-profits that have strong financial accountability, as evidenced by external credentials (such as ECFA for Christian organizations), internal audit results, and Boards that have outside directors with financial expertise.

- Invest in your passion and organizations you know well. You will be asked to donate to many different causes through your life, and may feel guilty when you turn someone down. My biggest donation mistakes were made when I gave without focus or a full knowledge of the organizations that were receiving my contributions. Many companies have learned to focus their giving in a particular area, such as children, illiteracy, homelessness or hunger. When asked to donate to other causes, they can readily decline, as they have already specified their area of focus. Individuals should follow the same strategy. Figure out what you are passionate about. Maybe you went through a period when you didn't have enough to eat and are, therefore, interested in reducing hunger. Or, you have cared for an elderly person and want to help indigent seniors. Look for an organization that serves your passion and volunteer there. Work on the front line, so you can see how the non-profit serves the community. Interview the leadership to hear their vision, and see how effectively the vision is implemented. Serve on the Board, if you have skills in that area. Check out the financials to ensure money is used efficiently. Then, you can invest your time, talent and money with passion, knowing you are filling a need that satisfies you internally and others externally.
- Talk to your spouse. If you are married or have a significant other, you should discuss your giving with your spouse. Hopefully, you can find a cause that you are both passionate about, and contribute time and money together. If not,

you can still be a good balance for the other person when it comes to emotional giving or spending too much time on a cause, to the detriment of other responsibilities.

▸ Be careful of multi-year pledges. If you meet with professional fundraisers, you will often find you are asked to pledge a certain amount for multiple years. The conversation usually starts with your willingness to give a one-time amount, say $1,000. The fundraiser will then ask, "Would you be willing to give $1,000 a year for the next three years?" If you say no, you may then be asked, "Would you give $500 a year for the next three years?" Many people will agree, thinking this is a better deal, as there is less money paid upfront and the organization ultimately gets more money. The problem with this is that your situation or the receiving organization can change during those three years. New leadership may take over that has a different vision, or you may find out that your money was not used well. Then you are caught in a position of either giving unwillingly to keep your word or breaking your promise and walking away from the pledge that you made. The best approach is to give the amount of money you want to give at that time and reject a multi-year pledge. Instead, give annually, in an amount dictated by your situation and view of the organization.

▸ Specify special gifts. If you are supporting a non-profit, you should consider giving an ongoing amount to help pay for its operating costs, and then special contributions to support one-time spending, such as buildings. When you give a special contribution, it is best to designate how you want the money spent. Most organizations would prefer to spend the money as they see fit; however, we have been disappointed to find out a special contribution was used for ongoing expenses or unbudgeted extras that didn't move the organization forward. It is best for both the organization and donor to determine in advance how a special gift will be used to prevent any unwelcome surprises.

 Action Points

- ► Plan your giving as part of your budget.
- ► Give to causes you are passionate about.
- ► Do your homework to make sure your donations are not wasted.
- ► Agree with your spouse about where to give.
- ► Don't make multi-year pledges.
- ► Designate your giving.

 Payoff

Your money put to good use for a cause you believe in!

4. Sunny Skies

I violated the Noah rule: Predicting rain
doesn't count; building arks does.
— WARREN BUFFETT

When I led Epcot® theme park, we opened four major attractions, including Mission: SPACE! and Soarin'. Mission: SPACE! was the centerpiece of a national marketing campaign that focused on Epcot, and Soarin' was the key element in a strategy to take successful attractions from one Disney park (in the case of Soarin', Disney's California Adventure) and replicate them in other parks. When new attractions are launched, Disney typically has a "press event" with media from around the world invited for several days to interview executives and preview new products.

A highlight of the press event is the opening ceremony for new attractions, with Walt Disney Imagineering and Walt Disney Entertainment developing elaborate productions that include music, celebrities, characters and executives. For the Mission: SPACE! ceremony, we had a "Rocket Man" with a jetpack fly over the new attraction. For Soarin', the Imagineers created clouds on the ground and had a young boy fly through the clouds while the celebrity narrator, Patrick Warburton, welcomed the new experience.

Months in advance of press events, the teams would present their plans for my review. We would focus on operational issues, such as rehearsal schedules, guest impact, and safety. The one question I always learned to ask was, "What is the rain plan?"

Invariably, all the events assumed good weather, and my question would elicit worried looks and shrugged shoulders. "I guess we'll just have Mickey cut a ribbon at the entrance to the ride," was a usual, not very satisfactory, response.

Most people don't think about having a rain plan. Like the Imagineers, they assume the skies will be sunny, and nothing will interfere with their plans. But, unfortunately, life is not like that. People lose jobs, get sick, have to replace the air conditioner, need to take care of elderly parents, or lose a loved one. Many are devastated when this occurs, but the outcome is considerably better for those with a rain plan.

While you shouldn't dwell on all the bad things that can happen to you, you should certainly consider them and have a plan for what you will do to respond. Everyone should have 90–180 days of living expenses saved in a guaranteed bank account to support them in the event of a job loss. You should have a replacement fund for major appliances and cars, as you know they will wear out. You should discuss with your spouse what you will do if one of you dies, and make sure all your IRAs and life insurance policies have the correct beneficiaries. If you have older parents, you should determine the plan for their care if they become incapacitated. You obviously can't prepare for every contingency, but with some pre-thought and planning, you can reduce the impact when the rains come, and excel in your response.

 ## Action Points

- ▸ Ask, "What is the Rain Plan?"
- ▸ Have an emergency fund for living expenses.

- Create a replacement fund for your car and house maintenance.
- Think about the major "bad" things that can happen to you and have a plan to deal with them.

 ## Payoff

When the rains come, they won't sink your boat!

5. The 100 Item Club

We spend money we don't have, to buy things we
don't need, to impress people we don't like.
— WILL ROGERS

I recently read an article about the "100 Item Club." Members of this club agree to only own a total of 100 items. In this case, an "item" means things like a spoon, cup, plate, toothbrush, belt, shirt, etc. It is not clear if a pair of shoes or socks is one item or two, but in the strictest definition, I assume you would have to count each sock or shoe separately. At first, I thought the concept of limiting yourself to this degree was crazy. But, as I considered it further, there is a simplicity and discipline that is appealing.

We all need to learn how to keep our lifestyles in check. Our marketing and sales-driven culture is based on creating unnecessary dissatisfaction and desire. Before watching a television ad, you may have no idea that you "need" a pick-up truck or that you will be able to go out with a beautiful woman if you just drink a particular kind of beer. Advertisements play to particular fears, like having body odor or bad breath, or running out of money in old age. Many are focused on sexuality and being appealing to others. All promise to solve your problems (sometimes real, most often created) if you just buy a particular item or service. People get sucked into the spending cycle— buying something to make them feel better about themselves, getting initial pleasure and then a let down, and then buying something else that ultimately disappoints.

There are several ways to break the cycle. First, you have to differentiate wants from needs. You may *want* something, but do you really *need* it? More stuff leads to more hassles. One of the worst purchases I ever made was a waterskiing boat. When I left Disney, I promised to buy my children, who were then teenagers, a boat. After nine years in the Navy, I had had enough of boats to last me for my lifetime. But, I felt a little guilty that they would no longer be able to have Disney experiences (although Hilton stays were a great replacement!). The boat added major complexity to our lives, with trailering, maintenance, storage, insurance, fueling, cleaning, etc. It seemed like every time we planned a lake day, the boat didn't work. It was an expensive burden.

As I thought about it, most new items that we buy are like the boat. We get the latest electronic gadget, then have to spend time figuring out how to make it work. If it is a computer, we have to do constant software upgrades or download new anti-virus software. Smartphones can be useful, but can also be a time-sink and take away from personal interactions. The pleasure versus stress trade-off is often out of whack, and your "wants" become encumbrances.

Second, if you do need it, think about buying it used. Marketers will tell you one of the most enticing words to put into an advertisement is "new." People assume new is better and more desirable. Yet, there is often nothing wrong with "used." I own a BMW and talked to one of their technicians while waiting on my car. I asked him about the most reliable cars, and he said the best strategy is to buy a car that is a few years old. He said, "It's crazy that owners trade in their cars when they are three years old. That is just when all the bugs have been fixed. BMW is constantly upgrading the software in their vehicles, and the early years are when you have the most upgrades." He recommended buying a pre-owned car that was a few years old, both for the value and the lowest maintenance requirements.

Third, don't automatically buy a bigger house when your income increases. You should actually also consider renting rather than buying. We have lived in the same home for over seventeen years. We have been very tempted to trade up to a larger home or one on a lake. But, we have also been very thankful as we have watched friends become "house poor" or even lose their homes when the economy and home prices turned down. By living in the same home for a long period, we have withstood real estate market changes and kept our taxes low. With that said, we should have considered renting rather than purchasing our home. Most studies show you should never buy a home unless you are certain to live in it for more than seven years, or you will lose money when compared to renting. As I look back, there is no question that we should have rented our homes instead of buying in the first decade of our marriage. Nancy and I moved eleven times in our first thirteen years. We purchased two homes during that time. When we moved to England, we had to rent out our home in Cleveland. Had we not purchased, we likely would have lived in larger homes, simplified our lives significantly, and been better off financially.

If you want to dampen your inclination toward a materialistic lifestyle, work in a homeless shelter or, better yet, travel to a third world country and see how most of the world's population lives. Most Americans have two homes and don't even realize it. An American family adopted a boy who lived in a slum in South America. When they got to their home, the boy put his few belongings in the garage and started to set up his bed there. His adoptive parents asked him what he was doing, and he said he was putting his things in their "home." They explained to him that this was the garage, and then opened the door to his home. "So, all Americans have two homes?" he asked, with an amazed look on his face. We don't often think about having two homes, but to most people in other countries, the idea of storing your cars in an enclosed, covered space is extravagant.

Keeping your lifestyle in check provides simplicity, freedom from debt, an ability to give more to help others, and a fabulous example for your children—all part of a surpassing lifestyle.

 ## Action Points

Before making any purchase, ask:
- ▸ Do I really need this, or am I being manipulated to buy it?
- ▸ Will this make my life simpler or more complex?
- ▸ Should I buy it used?
- ▸ Should I rent rather than buy?

Don't buy a bigger house just because you can afford it.

 ## Payoff

Financial freedom and a simpler, easier life.

CHAPTER 2

Health Beyond Measure

As I see it, every day you do one of two things:
build health or produce disease in yourself.
— ADELLE DAVIS

Look to your health; and if you have it, praise God and value
it next to conscience; for health is the second blessing that
we mortals are capable of; a blessing money can't buy.
— IZAAK WALTON

Health nuts are going to feel stupid someday,
lying in hospitals dying of nothing.
— REDD FOXX

Health is worth more than learning.
— THOMAS JEFFERSON

Dear friend, I pray that you may enjoy good health and that all
may go well with you, even as your soul is getting along well.
— BIBLE, 3 JOHN 1:2

I F YOU ARE NOT HEALTHY, everything else in life becomes
a lesser priority. And, if you are healthy and vibrant, you'll
have the energy and desire to excel in all the other areas of your
life. Preserving health is key to living a great, surpassing life.

25

Many of us know the things we should do, the habits we should form, to have a healthy life. Unfortunately, our society does everything possible to make us sick, particularly in the marketing of unhealthy foods, a sedentary lifestyle, frenetic personal schedules, and abuse of products like alcohol and cigarettes. The following sections should encourage you to challenge these norms, with practical ways to live a healthy and fruitful life.

6. The Magic Food

The sovereign invigorator of the body is exercise, and of all exercises walking is best. Habituate yourself to walk very far.
— THOMAS JEFFERSON

To get back to my youth, I would do anything in the world, except take exercise, get up early or be respectable.
— OSCAR WILDE

If there were an incredible food that reduces stress, energizes creative thinking, lowers blood pressure, enhances sleep, promotes longevity and manages weight, would you buy it? Of course!

Unfortunately, there is no such food. But, you can get all of these benefits and more from physical exercise. Numerous studies have demonstrated the clear advantages from thirty to sixty minutes daily of aerobic, strength and flexibility exercises. By putting exercise into your daily routine, you will feel and perform much better. The key is to make exercise a part of your weekly schedule. It is an appointment for yourself, to keep you healthy and at peak performance.

At the Naval Academy, all midshipmen are required to do sports throughout the school year. From that experience, I learned the discipline and value of scheduling workouts into my daily routine. I've tried morning, lunchtime and evening workouts and I believe the best time is the morning, before work. Otherwise, it becomes too easy to skip due to work requirements or fatigue.

I'm also an efficiency nut, and it is much more efficient (and better for your skin) to take only one shower per day. I work out at home, rather than a gym, to save travel time and also limit my excuses ("Can't go to the gym today because it is raining, snowing, etc."). Others may have a different point of view and go to a gym for greater accountability by joining a class or meeting a workout partner.

My two biggest challenges with maintaining a workout schedule are early breakfasts and travel. I'm sorry, but if I have a seven AM breakfast, I'm not getting up at five to work out. Business travel is tough, with irregular hours and packed days. I have light and compact workout clothes and sneakers for travel and bring them on most trips. With my goal of five workouts/week, I use Saturdays and Sundays as make-up days for any exercise days missed during the week.

Your exercise routine should include at least thirty minutes of hard aerobic exercise. I use a stairclimber or elliptical trainer to minimize the impact on my knees. I really like the stairclimber because you can't "cheat" on the speed—if you stop stepping, the pedals go to the floor. Rowing is also a great workout, as you exercise your arms as well as your legs.

Interval training gives the most efficient workout. With interval training, you vary the speed, going as fast as you can for thirty seconds every three minutes. This enhances your recovery speed, and also helps prepare you for the real world of intense, immediate activity.

Strength and flexibility are other important aspects of your routine. While you can use weights and machines, exercises that use your own weight, like pushups, allow you to work out anywhere, including your hotel room. Slow counts (lowering and raising to a count of 5) and limited reps (10–12, one to two times) provide more benefits than fast, multiple repetitions. Flexibility exercises improve both your aerobic and strength workouts, and should be done after warming up, not before.

While I am doing my aerobic exercise (elliptical and stair-climber), I read and think. My reading is usually from the Bible, and I ponder the verses. I also think about business problems and often come up with great solutions. When I worked at British Petroleum, I regularly used their fitness center during lunchtime. While I was there, I came up with the idea for a new financing technique that saved the company millions of dollars and received an innovation award. As I received the award, the company president asked me how I came up with the idea, and I told him it was on the rowing machine in the fitness center. In his proper British accent, he replied, "Well then, you must row 'the pond' (the British euphemism for the Atlantic Ocean) and generate many more ideas!"

You should consider getting a personal trainer to help determine an optimal exercise routine for you. Proper techniques are critical for effective workouts, and a trainer can correct your form. Once you get the workouts and form determined, you can decide whether to keep the trainer or work out on your own.

If you don't currently have an exercise program, this should be one of your first surpassing decisions. Start now, and see the difference in your energy and self-confidence.

 ## Action Points

- ▸ Set up your daily schedule to include exercise, preferably first thing in the morning.
- ▸ Strive to exercise five days per week, using Saturday and Sunday as make-up days for missed workouts during the week.

- Take a lightweight exercise outfit on business trips to maintain your routine.
- Treat exercise time as an appointment with yourself, and use it to clear your mind and solve problems.

 Payoff

More energy, confidence, health and vibrancy!

7. Submerged For 70 Days

*Everyone has a doctor in him or her; we just have to help
it in its work. The natural healing force within each one
of us is the greatest force in getting well. Our food should
be our medicine. Our medicine should be our food.*
— HIPPOCRATES

Food is an important part of a balanced diet.
— FRAN LEBOWITZ

I watched as the last crate of fresh vegetables went down the
hatch into my submarine. We were preparing to leave on our
ten-week patrol—submerged for 70 days with no new supplies.
We would run out of fresh salads, milk and eggs after about
a week, and from then on, everything would be frozen, dried
or canned.

I had a terrible diet growing up. Despite my mother's best
intentions, I was a "meat and potatoes" person, who rarely ate
salad and vegetables and had only a few favored fruits. I loved
thick slices of roast beef, fried chicken, fried shrimp, whole
milk, ice cream, soda and candy. Fortunately, I was active or I
might have suffered from childhood obesity.

When I became a submarine officer, I suddenly valued fresh
fruits and vegetables much more, as "absence makes the heart
grow fonder." I couldn't wait to get back to port and have real
eggs, milk and, yes, even salad for me.

I later discovered the idea of eating colorful foods. My
doctor told me a simple test to determine if you are eating correctly is to look at the amount of color on your plate. Healthy

foods have color, like green and red peppers. Less healthy foods are white, like white bread, mashed potatoes, and sugar. It's easy, but effective. I've also weaned myself off fried foods. I discovered that I couldn't taste the food through the batter and grease. Try the experiment of tasting two different fried foods, like chicken and shrimp, with your eyes closed. I'll bet you find it's hard to tell which food is which. Grilling, broiling, pan sautéing, or baking is much healthier and allows the true food taste to shine through.

What you drink has a huge impact on nutrition. Soda is one of the worst things you can put in your mouth. A sixteen ounce soda has sixteen teaspoons of sugar. Imagine getting a big cup of coffee and putting sixteen sugar packets in it! Diet sodas contain artificial sweeteners with unknown effects. All sodas contain phosphoric acid that reduces calcium absorption, and people (especially teenagers) replace milk consumption with soda. Calcium depletion results in bone weakness and stress fractures. My decision point on soda came when I led Epcot. During engineering reviews, I would see thick, cast-iron drain pipes that had eroded away because of soda. I thought, "That can't be good for your body." After that, water, coffee, tea, skim milk and fruit juices (including wine) became my drinks of choice.

Breakfast is the most important meal of the day, yet less than half of Americans eat breakfast. Countless studies have shown the benefits of having a protein-filled, low carbohydrate breakfast, including greater morning energy, fewer food cravings, and higher mental agility. High performance organizations like the military teach recruits to get up and have breakfast. There are various excuses about skipping breakfast, but they are flimsy. It's an easy meal, with foods like Greek yogurt, hard boiled eggs, smoothies, whole wheat cereal or toast, and bananas. The small amount of time it takes to prepare and eat breakfast is more than recovered by higher productivity in the morning. If you don't currently eat breakfast, start now and see how much better you feel and perform.

While entire books have been written about nutrition, just applying these three easy ideas—eat colorful foods, don't drink soda and eat breakfast—will improve your health, help you manage your weight and improve your productivity. Put them into practice today and start living the surpassing life.

 ## Action Points

▶ Replace "white" foods with colorful foods.
▶ Grill or broil instead of frying.
▶ Stop drinking soda and start drinking water.
▶ Eat breakfast every day.

 ## Payoff

Easier weight management, more energy and a healthier, longer life!

8. Sleep Deprived

Not being able to sleep is terrible. You have the misery of
having partied all night . . . without the satisfaction.
— LYNN JOHNSTON

To achieve the impossible dream, try going to sleep.
— JOAN KLEMPNER

My mom was one of those people who could consistently excel on five hours of sleep per night. She would stay up until one AM watching the Johnny Carson show.[4] Then, she would be up at six AM to catch the morning shows.

Most people can't make it on five hours of sleep: in fact, sleep researchers believe only 5 percent of the population has this genetic trait. However, many try. Americans are in a perpetual state of fatigue. The "work hard, play hard" mentality results in guilt for any time spent sleeping, even though the right amount of sleep results in greater creativity and productivity. The average American gets less than the recommended seven to nine hours of sleep per night, even though studies have shown that getting less than six hours of sleep results in a 12 percent higher probability of premature death and can cause obesity, high blood pressure and diabetes.[5]

People who are sleep-deprived are also unpleasant to be around—irritable, inattentive, depressed and unproductive. The best torture technique is severe sleep deprivation, as a subject

---

[4]   Younger readers can relate Johnny Carson to Jay Leno or David Letterman.
[5]   National Sleep Foundation, www.sleepfoundation.org

will say anything to be allowed to sleep, and there are no lasting physical or mental effects. Sustained periods without sleep result in hallucinations. I personally experienced this during intense operations when I was in the Navy. Falling asleep at the wheel can kill as readily as drunk driving. You owe it to yourself and others to get enough sleep.

How do you ensure adequate sleep? Make an inviolable appointment with yourself to be in bed for eight hours per night, and then build the rest of your schedule around your sleep time. Don't let your spouse, children, dog, friends or work take away your sleep priority. Remember that they will all benefit if you get enough sleep. Thirty minutes prior to bedtime, turn off all screens (TV, computer, phone) and get ready for bed. You'll drift off to sleep and wake up ready to attack the day.

Have you dreaded Mondays, knowing that you will drag through the day and be especially tired in the afternoon? Poor Monday performance is frequently caused by sleep "bingeing" on the weekend. Instead of getting up at the normal weekday time of six or seven AM, many people use Saturdays and Sundays as an excuse to sleep until nine or ten AM. Waking up early on Monday confuses the body's clock (circadian rhythm) and results in a lousy day. If you keep your sleep hours consistent on the weekends by waking up within an hour of your normal weekday time, you'll skip the Monday blahs and get your week off to a strong start.

Naps can be highly productive. A twenty-minute "power nap" in the afternoon can propel you to greater productivity in the afternoon and evening. You can add to this with a "caffeine nap," in which you drink a cup of coffee before your nap. The coffee will take about twenty minutes to kick in, so you wake up refreshed and alert.

Although not recommended long term, if you are in a short-term crunch period at school or work, try poly-phasic sleep. With poly-phasic sleep, you get six hours of sleep at night (say, midnight to six AM) and take a twenty-minute nap at around two PM. The net result is an extra one and a half hours of work time daily, albeit with some productivity reduction during the other hours.

Sleep cycles get destroyed on international trips. Having traveled around the world, I've found jet lag kills productivity. The two best solutions for jet lag are sunlight and melatonin. Sunlight resets the body's clock. Unfortunately, many business-people fly to an international city and immediately attend meetings in darkened, windowless conference rooms. Their world remains upside down and they zone out during presentations. The best strategy is to get as much daylight as possible. At a minimum, demand to meet in a room with windows and keep the blinds open.

Melatonin is a proven jet lag cure. In clinical research studies, a 5 mg dose of melatonin taken at the target bedtime of the destination decreased jet lag from flights crossing five or more time zones. The study recommended doing this at least two days, and noted that the benefits are greater for more time zones and when flying eastward.[6]

I often have trouble sleeping the first night in a hotel. I'm usually jet lagged or anticipating the next day's meetings. I recently discovered the trick of taking an ice bath right before going to bed. Fill the bathtub with cold water, add ice from the ice bucket and submerge yourself for ten minutes (or as long as

---

[6]   Herxheimer A, Petrie KJ. Melatonin for the prevention and treatment of jet lag. *Cochrane Database of Systematic Reviews* 2002, Issue 2. Art. No.: CD001520. DOI: 10.1002/ 14651858.CD001520.

you can stand it!). You'll fall asleep as soon as your head hits the pillow and stay asleep until the alarm sounds.

Adequate sleep is a life necessity and critical to a surpassing life.

 Action Points

- Build your daily schedule around getting eight hours of sleep per night.
- Turn off all screens thirty minutes before bed.
- Sleep consistent hours—don't binge on weekends.
- Use power or "caffeine" naps to improve afternoon productivity.
- Try poly-phasic sleep during crunch times.
- Adjust to jet lag with daylight and melatonin.
- Take an ice bath to get a deeper sleep.

 Payoff

Greater creativity and productivity, a more pleasant personality, the energy to enjoy life!

9. Zipper Stripes

For the drunkard and the glutton shall come to poverty.
— BIBLE, PROVERBS 23:21

When I read about the evils of drinking, I gave up reading.
— HENNY YOUNGMAN

Alcohol can destroy individuals, families, careers, reputations and lives. Often the most successful people pursue a self-destructive path of alcohol or drug abuse. Work stress, unmet expectations, loneliness or guilt are assuaged with another drink until abuse becomes habitual. Social pressure to be "part of the crowd" can also result in drinking to excess.

While a glass of red wine at dinner has shown some potential health benefits, alcohol abuse destroys health, through liver cirrhosis, cardiomyopathy (heart disease), peripheral neuropathy (nerve damage), and brain shrinkage. Alcoholics often have poor nutrition and sleep disruption, compounding these issues.

The social effects of alcohol abuse can be immediate and life threatening. Alcohol consumption reduces self-control and can cause people to say and do things that cause pain and regret. In the work setting, coworkers can be harassed or abused, bosses offended and clients lost. At home, excessive consumption can result in failed marriages, domestic violence or child abuse. Drunken driving in the best case leads to arrest and jail, and, in the worst case, destruction and death.

In the Navy, several divisions that I led had enlisted men with alcohol abuse issues. These men would perform well for a period and get promoted to the next rank, which would earn them an additional stripe in rank. Invariably, they would go on a binge, get into trouble, be disciplined and lose a stripe. The cycle would repeat. We used the expression "zipper stripes," telling them they should put their stripes on with a zipper so they could add and remove them more easily.

If you suspect you may be an alcoholic, get professional help from a doctor. If you have a predilection toward alcohol abuse, consider the following:

▸ Go "cold turkey" and don't drink any alcohol. Many people do not drink at all today for various reasons—to prevent weight gain, for religious beliefs, to save money, or because they get a headache or don't like the taste. It is culturally acceptable to say no and you should not feel you have to drink to fit in.

▸ Don't hang out with people who drink. You will emulate your friends, and if they drink (particularly in excess), you will too.

▸ Get a friend (preferably not your spouse) to hold you accountable. Tell your friend you need their help, and ask them to quiz you (and your spouse) on a weekly basis about your alcohol use. It's better to have a friend do this than your spouse, as your spouse can come across as nagging.

▸ Write down your commitment to not drink and then list all the benefits (how much money you will save, better you will feel, problems you'll prevent). When you feel the urge to have a drink, pull out your written commitment and benefits.

Moderation in all things, especially alcohol, leads to a positive, healthy, surpassing life.

Action Points

- ▶ Don't succumb to social pressure—drink alcohol in moderation or not at all.
- ▶ Monitor how much you drink and have someone hold you accountable.
- ▶ If you have an alcohol problem, get help.
- ▶ If your friends drink to excess, get new friends.
- ▶ Put your commitment to not drink in writing and carry it with you.

 ## Payoff

Better health, no alcohol-related accidents or liability, no regrets!

10. My One Pleasure in Life

I phoned my dad to tell him I had stopped smoking.
He called me a quitter.
— STEVEN PEARL

I have never smoked a cigarette in my life, and I don't ever plan to have one. Smoke and lungs are not a good combination. Cigarettes are highly addictive (just look at people who stand outside in freezing weather to have a smoke) and incredibly expensive. Over a lifetime, a pack-a-day smoker will spend over $100,000 in cigarettes, and considerably more when including health and life insurance premiums and cleaning bills. Recently, some companies, especially hospitals, have refused to employ people who smoke, further limiting smokers' ability to get jobs or advance.

The American Heart Association states that cigarette smoking is the "single most alterable risk factor for heart disease, accounting for 400,000 deaths annually." One-half of smokers will be killed by their habit, and a person in his or her twenties will live one-quarter less than a non-smoker of the same age. From a societal standpoint, the medical costs related to cigarette smoking exceed $50 billion per year.

Despite the proven physical and economic impacts, 3,000 teenagers start smoking every day, resulting in over one million new smokers every year. A key determinant of whether young people smoke is whether their parents smoke. Dr. Stephen E. Gilman of the Harvard School of Public Health in Boston found that children who were younger than twelve when their parents were active smokers were 3.6 times more likely to smoke as children of non-smokers.

I remember counseling a young Navy petty officer in one of my submarine divisions. He had significant financial issues, and I was helping him budget his money. I told him he could quit smoking and use those funds to pay down his debt. He said, "Mr. Rex, smoking is my one pleasure in life." What a sad commentary and indication of the addictive power of nicotine.

If you consider exercise as a magic food to prolong life, smoking is a destructive habit that destroys life. Here are the negative effects of cigarettes on your heart and blood vessels:

- Reduces good (HDL) cholesterol, while increasing bad (LDL) cholesterol and oxidizing the LDL into a more toxic form
- Increases heart rate and blood pressure
- Causes spasms of the heart arteries, and makes them thicker and stiffer
- Raises insulin resistance
- Increases fibrinogen, a protein that causes blood clots
- Impairs cells lining blood vessels

One pack per day smokers increase their risk of heart attack by six times for women and three times for men, while markedly increasing the chance of stroke. Smoking will cause you to age prematurely, and dramatically increase your risk of cancer and other diseases, including lung, bladder, stomach, pancreas, esophagus, larynx, mouth and cervical cancer, along with emphysema and peptic ulcer disease.

There is no "pleasure" in that. There are no upsides or benefits to smoking—it is an addictive, expensive, life-robbing habit. If you have never smoked, don't start. And, if you are a smoker, quit. It isn't easy (70 percent of smokers would like to quit, 30 percent try in a given year, and 2.5 percent succeed), but by either going "cold turkey" or using nicotine patches or gum, you can break the habit. You owe it to yourself, your family and society to quit. You will be amazed at the benefits and improvement in your life.

 ## Action Points

- ▶ Understand the cost of smoking, both financially and in terms of your health.
- ▶ If you are not a smoker, don't start. If you are a smoker, quit.
- ▶ If you are a parent, quit, or you risk raising children who are also smokers.

 ## Payoff

A longer, healthier life with nicer teeth, fresher breath, and much more money!

CHAPTER 3
Honor Beyond Measure

Character is power; it makes friends, draws patronage and support, and opens the way to wealth, honor and happiness.
— JOHN HOWE

Then the other administrators began searching for some fault in the way Daniel was handling his affairs, but they couldn't find anything to criticize. He was faithful and honest and always responsible.
— BIBLE, DANIEL 6:4

I T IS SO SAD when you see someone destroy their life and, often, the lives of their families, employees and even entire communities through unlawful, dishonest or unethical behavior. The newspapers provide daily examples, such as Bernie Madoff (massive pyramid scheme), Eliot Spitzer (caught with a prostitute) and Ken Lay (CEO of Enron, a $100 billion company that went bankrupt due to accounting fraud). You look back and think, "What a waste. These were talented, intelligent people who could have had a major beneficial impact on society. Yet, because they lacked integrity, they brought doom on themselves and those around them."

On the other hand, people who live upright lives are often not featured in the media. Yet, they enjoy a wonderful life and

44

have a huge, positive influence on society. Surpassing living goes beyond the minimum of following the letter of the law. It cultivates honorable, ethical, responsible living, and celebrates the rewards of an honest lifestyle.

11. The *New York Times* Test

Virtue makes us aim at the right mark, and practical
wisdom makes us take the right means.
— ARISTOTLE

As a Naval Academy graduate, it kills me to have to give credit to our rival school, West Point, for anything. However, I like West Point's very simple and understandable Honor Code: "A cadet will not lie, cheat or steal, or tolerate those who do." I wish every person in America, and even the world, lived like this. Think about all the heartache, broken relationships, prison sentences and financial failures that could be avoided. Of course, it would have other effects, like a huge reduction in lawyers, accounting firms, security companies and private detectives. On an individual level, we would have much less shame, guilt, deception, suspicion and animosity.

While we have little control over others, we can choose to live this way ourselves. When confronted with the temptation to lie about a situation, cheat on expense reports or taxes, or steal from companies or partners, the simple statement "I will not lie, cheat or steal" should come to mind.

Sometimes we may believe there is a "gray zone" and are unsure about what is acceptable. In such cases, I use the *New York Times* test. The *New York Times* test asks, "If this action was on the cover of the *New York Times*, would you be ok with it?" I look at everything I say, write and do through the lens of this test. I have deleted many emails that I wrote, often in anger, that failed the NYTT. With the speed and ease of electronic communication, you have to assume that anything you write can be quickly shared to a broad audience. Thus, you need to be clear and honest, and consider how an outside reader would respond to your words. And, put it on the cover of the *New York Times*, to decide if it would make you and your family proud or embarrassed.

Preventing even the potential appearance of impropriety ensures that your honor is protected. Billy Graham would not be alone with a woman that was not his wife, even in a car or elevator—a third person would join them. His precaution was wise many years ago, and is even more so today, given the intense scrutiny and almost immediate sentencing by the media of anyone accused of improper behavior. Billy Graham's "rule of three," offices with glass panels, and keeping your calendar updated so you can recall your whereabouts on a particular day are all good safeguards for potential false accusations.

Action Points

- Adopt the dictum that you "will not lie, cheat or steal, or tolerate those who do."
- Before you say, write or do something, consider whether you want it to be on the cover of the *New York Times*.
- Delay before hitting "send" on an email, and re-read your message to make sure it is appropriate and could not be misconstrued.
- Protect yourself from even the appearance of impropriety and false accusations.

Payoff

A sterling reputation and much heartache prevented.

12. Blessing or Curse

When we lose one blessing, another is often most
unexpectedly given in its place.
— C. S. LEWIS

Surpassing living and leadership requires integrity. My greatest challenges in maintaining integrity often come when something bad happens to me. A poor performance, business reversal, or awkward social situation can motivate me to hedge the truth. When I am tempted this way, I remember the Chinese parable entitled "The Old Man and His Horse." What we may initially perceive as a "bad" situation may actually be a blessing, and losing our integrity defending it is a poor idea.

The Old Man and His Horse (a.k.a. Sai Weng Shi Ma)

Once there was an old man who lived in a tiny village. Although poor, he was envied by all, for he owned a beautiful white horse. Even the king coveted his treasure.

People offered fabulous prices for the steed, but the old man always refused. The man was poor and the temptation was great. But he never sold the horse.

One morning he found that the horse was not in his stable. All the village came to see him. "You old fool," they scoffed, "we told you that someone would steal your horse. You are so poor. It would have been better to have sold him. Now the horse is gone and you've been cursed with misfortune."

The old man responded, "Don't speak too quickly. Say only that the horse is not in the stable. That is all we know; the rest is judgment. If I've been cursed or not, how can you know? How can you judge?"

The people contested, "Don't make us out to be fools! We may not be philosophers, but great philosophy is not needed. The simple fact that your horse is gone is a curse."

The old man spoke again. "All I know is that the stable is empty, and the horse is gone. The rest I don't know. Whether it be a curse or a blessing, I can't say. All we can see is a fragment. Who can say what will come next?"

After fifteen days, the horse returned. He hadn't been stolen; he had run away into the forest. Not only had he returned, he had brought a dozen wild horses with him. Once again, the village people gathered around the woodcutter and spoke. "Old man, you were right and we were wrong. What we thought was a curse was a blessing. Please forgive us."

The man responded, "Once again, you go too far. Say only that the horse is back. State only that a dozen horses returned with him, but don't judge. How do you know if this is a blessing or not?"

"Maybe the old man is right," they said to one another. So they said little. But down deep, they knew he was wrong. They knew it was a blessing. Twelve wild horses had returned. With a little work, the animals could be broken and trained and sold for much money.

The old man had a son, an only son. The young man began to break the wild horses. After a few days, he fell from one of the horses and broke both legs. Once again the villagers gathered around the old man and cast their judgments.

"You were right," they said. "You proved you were right. The dozen horses were not a blessing. They were a curse. Your only son has broken both his legs, and now in your old age you have no one to help you. Now you are poorer than ever."

The old man spoke again. "You people are obsessed with judging. Don't go so far. Say only that my son broke his legs. Who knows if it is a blessing or a curse? No one knows. We only have a fragment. Life comes in fragments."

It so happened that a few weeks later the country engaged in war against a neighboring country. All the young men of the village were required to join the army. Only the son of the old man was excluded, because he was injured. Once again the people gathered around the old man, crying and screaming because their sons had been taken. They would never see their sons again.

"You were right, old man," they wept. "God knows you were right. This proves it. Your son's accident was a blessing. His legs may be broken, but at least he is with you. Our sons are gone forever."

The old man spoke again. "It is impossible to talk with you. You always draw conclusions. No one knows. Say only this. Your sons had to go to war, and mine did not. No one knows if it is a blessing or a curse. No one is wise enough to know. Only God knows."

Think about situations you have faced that you initially considered a curse and later became a blessing. Many of my friends who have had serious medical issues, such as cancer, tell me that their lives are much richer and more valuable to them now. After going through infertility and not knowing if we would be able to have biological children, my wife and I have an even deeper love for our son and twin daughters.

The opposite can occur, when a supposedly "good" situation turns bad. Most lottery winners will tell you winning a huge sum can end up being a curse rather than a blessing. One of my doctors won a major lottery and had to stop practicing medicine at a young age out of fear of lawsuits seeking his winnings. Although he was financially secure, the profession that he loved and spent years learning in schools and hospitals was no longer available to him.

As different events occur in your life, be slow to judge whether they are "good" or "bad." In fact, analyze the situation to see both the good and bad aspects. This valuable insight will help you maintain perspective and face the experience with honor and resilience.

Action Points

- ▶ Be slow to determine if something is "good" or "bad."
- ▶ Don't lie to cover up a perceived "bad" situation.
- ▶ Maintain a positive perspective, seeing both the potential benefits and challenges for every event that happens to you.

Payoff

Calmness in the midst of storms, wisdom, and resilience.

13. Volunteer

*I don't know what your destiny will be, but one thing I do
know: the only ones among you who will be really happy
are those who have sought and found how to serve.*
— ALBERT SCHWEITZER

*He who endeavors to serve, to benefit, and improve the
world, is like a swimmer who struggles against a rapid
current in a river lashed into angry waves by the winds.
Often they roar over his head, often they beat him
back and baffle him. Most men yield to the stress of the
current. Only here and there the stout, strong heart and
vigorous arms struggle on toward ultimate success.*
— ALBERT PIKE

*Dedicate some of your life to others. Your dedication will not
be a sacrifice. It will be an exhilarating experience because
it is an intense effort applied toward a meaningful end.*
— DR. THOMAS DOOLEY

The Bible tells us "To whom much is given, much is expected."
Some people read this from a financial perspective and give
money in proportion to their income or assets. Giving money
is great and generosity is a virtue. However, beyond money, we
have all been given significant gifts of skills and experiences
that we should expect to share with others. This happens by
volunteering our time.

People of honor and character volunteer, helping organizations and other people by contributing their time. Everyone can

do this, from the highest-level CEO to the retiree and even the unemployed. Organizations are always looking for volunteers to help in a variety of ways.

Volunteers have numerous benefits:

- A much greater familiarity with the organization
- An opportunity to improve things
- The ability to meet the people served by the organization
- A chance to do something different than their everyday work
- The knowledge that you are helping someone and making a significant difference in people's lives
- The opportunity to be on a team with other people who share your interest in helping others

Similar to when you give money, you should seek the following when you give the gift of your time:

- Find a cause you are passionate about. Don't regularly volunteer somewhere that doesn't interest you or it will be a chore, not a joy.
- Make sure your time is well-spent. If you find you are wasting your time, suggest that the organization improve their processes, or volunteer to help them get organized.
- Use your gifts and experiences—don't just do any job that you are assigned. If you love being with people, ask to volunteer in a position with high contact. If you love working with numbers, be on the finance team.
- Work with friends. You can build tremendous camaraderie and life-long relationships working together as volunteers.
- Work with your spouse or other family members. Many families serve together and create great memories. Parents

can leave a wonderful legacy of service by including their children at an early age.

In obituaries, you frequently find that the highlight of a person's life was volunteering and helping people. To achieve honor beyond measure, try serving others.

Action Points

- Find a place to volunteer your time and talents.
- Put thought into where you work, matching your passions with the organization.
- Know what situations make you happiest and invest your efforts there.
- Ask your friends and family to join you in your service.

Payoff

Helping others, huge personal satisfaction, the admiration of others.

14. Better Than Gold and Silver

Glass, china and reputation are easily
cracked, and never well mended.
— BENJAMIN FRANKLIN

A good name is more desirable than great riches;
to be esteemed is better than silver or gold.
— BIBLE, PROVERBS 22:1

At Epcot, I had a new executive assigned as my marketing person. I had never met him, and so I asked a few people about his reputation. Several people said, "He will set up meetings with you and never show up." I responded in disbelief and was told, "Just wait and see." My assistant set up our first introductory meeting. About an hour before he was supposed to meet me in my office, he called my assistant and said he had to reschedule because "something had come up." I remembered what I had been told about his reputation, but gave him the benefit of the doubt. Then, the same thing happened at our next scheduled time. After that, my assistant and I had a running contest to guess when he would cancel our meetings—a week out, day out, hour, or even sometimes after the meeting was supposed to start. That was his "reputation"—and not a good one.

All of us have reputations. People may describe you in positive terms—smart, ethical, creative, hard working—or negative ones, such as unintelligent, arrogant or irresponsible. Other terms might also be used, like a politician, a networker, a hothead or a team player. Having a favorable reputation is critical to business and personal success. Whenever I have seriously considered hiring someone for a job, I first ask others about their reputation. I know others have asked about my reputation before hiring me. Why is a good reputation more valuable than money? If you have a great deal of money and a bad reputation, you won't be able to get a job after the money runs out. If you have little money but a great reputation, you have the opportunity to make more money and build your fortune.

You build your reputation by following positive character traits, like perseverance, honesty, generosity, farsightedness and wise choices. You should always go beyond the minimum, striving to live a life above reproach. You probably have a good idea of potential weaknesses where you can be tempted to fall, such as alcohol, fraternization/sex, or money. For your particular problem areas, set up safeguards and accountability to protect yourself and others. Create a firm line with limits ("I will not drink any alcohol, under any circumstances.") and write it down, so you can refer to it when tempted. Envision the pain you can cause yourself and your family if you fall, and bring that vision to mind when you have to make a decision. If you do fall, admit it immediately and honestly.

Sadly, the smartest people are also the best in rationalizing poor choices ("one drink won't hurt," "everyone cheats on their taxes," "we'll just have a fun evening together—I deserve that, don't I?"). Once things start to go wrong, the smart person tries to "figure a way out" rather than just confessing, accepting the consequences and moving on, and often gets deeper and deeper in trouble until he or she take themselves down, as well as those around them. It is much better to "face the music" immediately then attempt to rationalize and deceive.

You must guard and defend your reputation when attacked. I always had good friends in the organizations where I worked who would tell me if someone had raised an issue regarding my character or reputation. It is sad that this is necessary, but the higher you rise in an organization, the more likely someone will attack your reputation. This is particularly true if, as in the biblical case of Daniel, they have nothing else to criticize.

In defending your reputation, you should first confront your accuser one-on-one. Relate what you have heard, and the accusations that have been made against you. If the person denies making the allegation, you should ask if they have made any other statements that could have been construed in this way. If they affirm their remarks, tell them to come to you directly in the future if they have an issue rather than going to others. Then pursue the issue with them to see if there might be any truth to their assertion, rather than rejecting it outright. Oftentimes we have blind spots when we look at our own behavior and there can be a "grain of truth" in an accusation. If, after honest appraisal, you believe you have still been unjustifiably challenged, you should explain why to your accuser. If the accuser cannot be convinced, you should set up another meeting and bring a second person with you who can listen and intercede on your behalf. Usually this will take care of the issue; however, you can always have more join you to bolster your argument.

It takes effort and discipline to create a great reputation, and consistent vigilance to preserve it. A great reputation leads to a great life, and surpassing living.

 ## Action Points

► Ask a person who will be honest with you about your reputation.

- Know your weaknesses and put in safeguards to protect yourself.
- Envision what failure looks like and establish firm boundaries in advance to keep you from temptation.
- Don't rationalize poor choices.
- Defend your reputation, confronting challenges in the right way.

 Payoff

A spotless reputation, greater opportunities, prevention of much heartache.

15. Twin Sons From Different Mothers

Consult your friend on all things, especially on those
which respect yourself. His counsel may then be useful
where your own self-love might impair your judgment.
— SENECA

When the character of a man is not clear
to you, look at his friends.
— JAPANESE PROVERB

Do not be misled: "Bad company corrupts good character."
— BIBLE, 1 CORINTHIANS 15:33

Do not make friends with a hot-tempered person,
do not associate with one easily angered.
— BIBLE, PROVERBS 22:24

There are three things that will shape your life: the events that happen to you, the people you associate with, and the books that you read. We have limited control over the first, and complete control over the latter two. We tend to emulate those who are around us. If your friends are smart, honest, generous, healthy, kind and cheerful, you will tend to follow their example.

You should try to associate with people who are equal to or better than you in character. Some people do the opposite so they can cultivate a feeling of superiority. But, this can have significant long-term consequences, particularly in the areas of ethics and integrity. We often look to friends to rationalize our own behavior and dishonest friends reinforce, rather than reduce, temptation.

I've been fortunate to have several best friends in my life, including Jim Lewis. Jim and I say that we are "twin sons from different mothers," a phrase that is especially apparent when you see us together, since Jim is African American and I am Caucasian. We have known each other for fifteen years, and share similar views on faith, family, friends, leadership and character. We live the phrase from Proverbs that "there is a friend who sticks closer than a brother." We can spend hours talking together about different topics. Often, the topics deal with making ethical decisions, protecting our reputations, and determining God's plan for our lives. We know that no topic is off-limits and that we can be brutally honest with each other. We also look out for each other and our families.

Do you have a friend like this in your life? We can easily deceive ourselves and need best friends to tell us when we are "smoking our own exhaust." These "honesty sessions" can prevent serious mistakes in our business lives, with our spouses or children, or in the community.

Best friends can hold you accountable, reducing your capacity to be tempted by your weaknesses. They can also "watch your back," letting you know if someone is attacking your reputation. And, if you are attacked, best friends can defend you, and get others to come to your defense.

Finally, best friends add a depth to life, with someone to share your greatest triumphs and your greatest sorrows. During tough times you have an encourager and, at the peak of success, someone who can bring you back to earth with a gentle landing.

As Francois de La Rochefoucauld stated, "A true friend is the greatest of all blessings, and that which we take the least care of all to acquire." To fully experience surpassing living, you need to do the work of acquiring the blessing of a best friend.

Action Points

- ▶ Review the people with whom you associate. Are they equal to or better than you in character? If not, you may be placed in a situation that drags you down rather than raising you up.
- ▶ Do you have a best friend who can keep you accountable? Is there someone who will tell you when you are "smoking your own exhaust"?
- ▶ Will someone tell you when your reputation is being attacked? Will they help you defend yourself?
- ▶ Are you the best friend to someone else?

Payoff

Protection of your honor, encouragement in hard times, a richer life.

CHAPTER 4

Relationships Beyond Measure

Treasure your relationships, not your possessions.
— ANTHONY J. D'ANGELO

When you build bridges you can keep crossing them.
— RICK PITINO

Two are better than one, because they have a good return for their labor: If either of them falls down, one can help the other up. But pity anyone who falls and has no one to help them up.
— BIBLE, ECCLESIASTES 4:9–10

CONSIDER YOUR RELATIONSHIPS for a moment. Are they strong and numerous? Do you have a great relationship with your spouse and children? How about your boss and co-workers? Do you have many business and community friendships?

If you fail in relationships, you fail in life.

People who want a surpassing life focus on building and maintaining relationships at multiple levels with many people. Even if you are an introvert, as I am, you can have a strong network of family and friends that enrich your life through surpassing living.

16. Tell Me Your Story

Do not protect yourself by a fence, but rather by your friends.
— CZECH PROVERB

A true friend knows your weaknesses but shows you
your strengths; feels your fears but fortifies your faith;
sees your anxieties but frees your spirit; recognizes
your disabilities but emphasizes your possibilities.
— WILLIAM ARTHUR WARD

One who has unreliable friends soon comes to ruin, but
there is a friend who sticks closer than a brother.
— BIBLE, PROVERBS 18:24

A friend loves at all times, and a brother
is born for a time of adversity.
— BIBLE, PROVERBS 17:17

How do you make friends? It sounds like a basic question, but for many people, making friends is difficult. You should look at your passions, and find people who have similar interests. This may be work, sports, children's activities, non-profits, church or other religious institution, or hobbies.

Since most people spend the majority of their day at work, this is an obvious place to develop relationships. If you have chosen to work for an ethical company (and if not, you should be looking for a new job), then hopefully other ethical people will be attracted to work there. In sports, you can fairly quickly ascertain a person's character and honesty. My wife and I have developed many friendships through our kids' activities (especially when you spend hours at the ball fields and basketball courts together), as well as church. Think about where you spend your time after work. If you spend it at home watching television, you are not very likely to meet anyone. If you frequent bars, you probably won't meet people who have the highest character. But, if you like art and volunteer evenings in an art museum, you're likely to meet people and develop friendships based on common interests.

I've found the best question to ask whenever you meet someone new is "Tell me your story." Everyone has a story and likes to talk about themselves. In hearing their story, I frequently find connections with my own story. The person may have grown up in the Northeast, as I did, or been in the military. Maybe they love Disney or have children of the same ages. Those connection points are the beginning of a relationship and potentially a great friendship.

You should try to have friends that are both younger and older than you. For older friends, look to those who have the type of life you would like to have at that age. For example, if you are a young, married couple without children, you might look to a couple who have children, or even empty nesters who have survived, and hopefully thrived, through the child-rearing years. Oftentimes, we only develop friendships with people around our age, which means they have the same experience (or ignorance) level that we do. If you have young children and all your friends have young children, no one will know any more about raising preschoolers than anyone else. But, if you have friends who are older, they can often share their learning and give you confidence in your parenting skills. Similarly at work, an older employee can help you better understand the corporate world, and more successfully navigate political and ethical challenges. By having younger friends, you can be a source of wisdom and encouragement for others and receive their enthusiasm and appreciation.

The right friends—diverse, ethical, younger, older—add a depth of life and joy to those living the surpassing life.

Action Points

- Your friends should have similar passions to you. Pursue your passions and look for people participating in those activities.
- Ask people to tell you their story and look for connection points.
- In addition to friends who are your age, have friends who are at younger and older life stages.
- Share your life with your friends and encourage them to do the same with you.

Payoff

Lifelong friendships, greater wisdom during each life stage, encouragement and a joyful life.

17.　Playing Favorites

Rejoice in your special talents, and recognize others.
— C. S. LEWIS

*But I also want you to think about how this keeps
your significance from getting blown up into self-
importance. For no matter how significant you are,
it is only because of what you are a part of.*
— BIBLE, 1 CORINTHIANS 12:19

Diversity and inclusion is a significant theme at Disney parks and resorts. The rallying cry used by Disney is R.A.V.E.—Respect, Appreciate and Value Everyone. I really like this message, as it captures the idea that every person is important and makes a difference. As you live out the idea of respecting, appreciating and valuing everyone that you meet, you will develop strong relationships of mutual admiration. It pains me to watch a person smile and greet a fellow traveler at the airport, but ignore the custodian as if he was not there. We all have a tendency to judge a person's value and only interact with people who have an equal or greater "value" than us. And some actually demean people who are perceived as having less value.

I wasn't supposed to play favorites as the leader of Epcot. But, I have to admit that I did have a favorite group of Cast Members—the Custodial team. This team was very proud of the work that they did every day, twenty-four hours a day, 365 days a year, keeping Epcot spotless. I tried to attend many Custodial pre-shift meetings. When I did, you could hear a buzz around the room that the Vice President was there. I would often start the meetings by asking the group, "Who is more important—me or you?" I would go on to say that if I were gone for a month, very few Epcot Guests would notice. It might impact our longer-range plans and there may be a few small hits but, overall, the park would keep running well. However, if the Custodial team was gone for a day, imagine what would happen—trash bins overflowing, restrooms filthy, kitchens unsanitary. So, who is more important?

In 2004, Richard Branson, the billionaire leader of the Virgin companies, had a reality television show entitled *The Rebel Billionaire: Branson's Quest for the Best.* Through a series of business and physical challenges, Branson eliminated contestants, with the final contestant winning the opportunity to lead one of Branson's companies, Virgin Worldwide. One episode featured a business presentation that the team had to create and then present to Branson. The team worked on the presentation and was told to go across town by limousine. One member of the team was the clear leader and was a favored candidate to win the ultimate prize. When the group arrived at the building exit, the limousine was not there. Finally it arrived. Words were exchanged with the limousine driver, everyone got in, and they arrived at their destination. Richard Branson was not in the presentation room, and the group was told to present to some of his executives. The favored candidate did a brilliant job presenting and answering questions. At the end, the door to the conference room opened and Richard Branson walked in, dressed in a chauffeur's uniform. He stared directly at the favored candidate and told him he would never run one of his companies. The picture then went to video of the interaction with the limousine driver, and showed the candidate berating the chauffeur, who was Richard Branson in disguise, for being late and stupid. "If this is how you treat someone who is serving you, you will not serve as a leader in the Virgin organization," said Branson. Branson saw that this young leader did not respect, appreciate and value everyone, and his relationships would suffer because of it.

I used to put on a Custodial costume and walk around Epcot, panning and brooming. It was as if I was invisible. I could talk to Guests, watch how managers interacted with Cast Members, and gauge the service of the operation much better than when people knew the VP was in the park. And, it sent a clear message to the Cast at Epcot that I believed every job and every person was important.

Are you known as a person who respects, appreciates and values everyone? If so, you will find people will want to know you and build relationships with you. On the other hand, if you tend to demean and belittle others, you'll lead a lonely and often bitter life. The Bible tells us that we should "in humility, consider others better than yourself."[7] If you approach people this way and express genuine interest in them, you can create strong relationships and a wonderful, surpassing life.

 Action Points

- ▶ Respect, appreciate and value everyone, especially those who serve you.

---

[7]   Bible, Philippians 2:3

- ▶ Get "in costume" and do other peoples' roles to understand their life.
- ▶ Consider others better than yourself.

 Payoff

Deeper relationships, greater respect and appreciation of others, a diverse and inclusive work and personal life.

18. Admiral Rickover

Gain a modest reputation for being unreliable
and you will never be asked to do a thing.
— PAUL THEROUX

Unless commitment is made, there are only
promises and hopes . . . but no plans.
— PETER DRUCKER

We all know people who are not committed. They put in the time and do enough to get by. They make promises, but don't follow through: "I'll take care of it!," they say, and then they don't. They disappoint others who were counting on them. And they continually make excuses for their broken promises.

There are others, though, who are always reliable. Their word is their bond, and their promises are sound. With others' trust, they build strong relationships and outstanding personal and professional reputations.

Admiral Hyman G. Rickover was the father of the nuclear navy. Today, we take nuclear-powered ships and submarines for granted. But, back in the early 1950s, it was considered crazy to put a nuclear reactor (which at that time was the size of a city block) on a ship, particularly a submarine. Through sheer force of will, Rickover made a nuclear submarine a reality, and the USS Nautilus launched in 1954. In all the years since, there has never been a reactor accident involving a US nuclear-powered ship. Admiral Rickover was asked during an interview what he expected from the officers in his nuclear power program. "My expectations are simple," he explained. "I expect them to get

70

the job done . . . or die trying." Some may see this as an extreme expectation of commitment. However, to Admiral Rickover, it was reasonable. Because, in his program, if you failed to get the job done—if you said you were going to do something and didn't—you could cause people to die.

Most of us don't work in nuclear power plants or have commitments that could lead to radioactive releases. But we do count on each other every day in myriad ways, and apparently small commitments can make a huge difference. Consider medical technicians and pharmacy attendants who can make life-threatening mistakes with procedures and drugs. Restaurant employees can create food safety issues. Tractor-trailer drivers can cause devastating accidents. A parent can take his or her eye off a child and destroy a family. Commitments are important, and your reputation for making good on your commitments will enhance or damage your relationships.

At work, we need to preserve our professional reputations by showing up at meetings we agree to attend and actively participating. As part of my reputation, I try to respond to every email and call within twenty-four hours. This shows that I value the messages that people send to me and attempt to get back to them in a timely manner. I don't necessarily resolve the issue within that time, but I can at least acknowledge their message and let them know when I will get back to them. When a team member brings something to my attention as their leader, I will try to fix it, in a demonstration of my commitment to them. If I can't fix it, I let them know why. I held many employee roundtables and would frequently be told that a manager had been told about a problem, but didn't do anything about it. The employees considered this a lack of commitment on the part of the manager, and they were right.

If you find yourself in a situation where you are overcommitted, unfocused and disappointing everyone, I suggest you take a day or weekend away to refocus and recommit. During that time, you should list all your commitments. Think about why you agreed to a particular commitment in the first place. Sometimes we agree to do something because no one else volunteers, or we don't want to disappoint someone, even though we are not really passionate about it. Other times, we continue to do something that should be delegated to someone else because "it's just easier if I do it." Determine the commitments that you are truly passionate about and get out or reduce your commitment for the others. You have to be willing to just say no or delegate it, even if it means you have to spend a little upfront time teaching someone else to do it. When you understand what you are doing and why, you'll be much more committed and motivated to accomplish your objective.

Another good practice if you are married is to do a weekly review of your commitments with your spouse. Set a time and sit down together to review the upcoming weeks. Make sure you both know about work, family or community events, and who is expected to attend what. This ensures that there are no "surprises," for example, when one spouse expects the other to take the children to school and the spouse has a breakfast meeting.

There have clearly been times when I've had to miss one of my children's events because of a work commitment. In those cases, I make sure to tell the child in advance that I can't attend and explain why. I also ensure that the next event for that child takes priority. Remember that you will always have your family, but you will not always have your work, and make your decisions accordingly.

By honoring your commitments at work, home and in your community, you will build and preserve the relationships that lead to a full and satisfying life.

 ## Action Points

- If you commit to attend a meeting, be there!
- Respond to all emails and calls in twenty-four hours.
- Get a day away, list all your commitments, and determine the ones you are passionate about.
- Delegate or eliminate commitments that no longer make sense.
- Do a weekly review of your commitments with your spouse.
- Make family commitments a priority.

 ## Payoff

An excellent professional and personal reputation, and strong relationships!

19. Can You Hear Me Now?

Listening, not imitation, may be the sincerest form of flattery.
— Dr. Joyce Brothers

A good listener is not only popular everywhere,
but after a while he gets to know something.
— Wilson Mizner

If you listened hard enough the first time, you
might have heard what I meant to say.
— Unknown

Opportunities are often missed because we are
broadcasting when we should be listening.
— Unknown

I am often asked, "What is the most important skill required for a leader?" While there are many potential answers—financial acumen, negotiations, planning, time management—my vote is "active listening."

Being an active listener is critical in all interpersonal relationships. Husbands and wives, parents and children, employers and employees, politicians and constituents—all benefit from active listening. As Ernest Hemingway said, "Most people never listen," which is why most people have poor relationships. The active listener is unique, especially in today's world, and this uniqueness translates into personal and professional excellence, with many strong relationships.

At employee roundtables, I would frequently hear the criticism, "My manager doesn't listen to me." When employees would come to see me with an issue, they would often say, "You really listened to me" at the end of our session. What was the difference between the interaction with their manager and the time with me? Active listening.

With active listening, you focus entirely on the other person, without distractions. The cell phone is put away, email notification is turned off, the computer screen is facing another direction and the door is shut. You have a note pad and pen, and are taking notes while the person talks. You paraphrase back to the speaker what they are saying to you: "So what I hear you telling me is . . ." "You are angry because . . ." "You believe your leader told you this, but did that." You encourage the person to speak, especially about their feelings: "Tell me more about this." "How did it make you feel when this happened?"

During the entire time, you are watching their body language to pick up non-verbal cues. Your body language is open and accepting (no crossed arms or peaked hands). You don't immediately jump into problem solving mode, but rather let the person fully explain the situation and how they feel about it. When the person is done, you paraphrase back the entire story using the notes that you took while they were speaking, and asking them whether you heard them correctly. After all that is complete, then you are ready to take the next step.

If the issue involves a conflict with a peer, your first question should be, "Have you discussed this with the person directly— one on one?" If they say no, then you direct them to do that first, or you will be put into the middle of the situation unnecessarily. Don't "take the monkey on your back" by agreeing to talk to the other person individually. If they say yes, then tell them to set up a meeting with the three of you together, so you get to hear both sides at once. Oftentimes, the person will go back and resolve the issue rather than set up a follow-up meeting.

If the issue involves conflict with someone else (their leader, for example) realize that there are always two sides to every story. I frequently made the mistake early in my life and career of only hearing one side and jumping to conclusions. After a few embarrassments, I've learned to seek the other side, usually finding truth is somewhere in the middle. Frank Tyger made the very accurate statement: "Listening to both sides of a story will convince you that there is more to a story than both sides." A good question to ask is: "What would the other person say if I asked him or her about what happened?"

You should determine if the person wants your help in solving the problem or just wanted you to listen to them. Men in particular are often guilty of trying to solve a problem when their spouse just wanted them to listen. Sometimes the speaker will tell you, "Thank you for listening to me. I feel much better now," and there is no further action required.

If the person is looking for a solution, a good place to start is to ask the person, "What do you think should happen in this situation?" This teaches people to try to solve problems for themselves rather than coming to you on every issue. He or she may already have a good solution and just need your help or encouragement to make it happen. Sometimes their proposed solution is impractical, and you need to explain why, and help them think of other options. While there are some things you will have to handle, the best solution is always one that the person can do himself. They get the satisfaction of solving a problem, and you don't get one more thing on your to-do list.

At the end of the meeting, you should restate any agreements and the agreed deadline. Then, document the agreement with a brief email that you complete while you are together, if possible. This ensures accountability for both of you.

The difference between passive and active listening is dramatic, and is as frustrating as a poor cell phone connection. Passive listeners are distracted, thinking about other things or planning their response before they have even heard the problem. Passive listeners don't repeat back what they hear and often misunderstand the speaker. Passive listeners don't take notes, so they appear uninterested and don't have a record of the meeting. They jump in to solve a problem they don't understand and create confusion and misunderstandings.

Active listeners focus on the problem and the person, picking up significant non-verbal cues. They listen to understand and confirm that their understanding is correct. They carefully document the conversation and refer back to their notes, enhancing their credibility with the speaker. They hold back on solving the problem, acting as a sounding board so the speaker can learn to solve their own problems. Their ultimate solutions are well grounded, thoughtful and tested, and of immense help to the speaker. Active listeners are considered respectful and wise, and people want to meet and know them. Their relationships are bountiful and rich, an excellent measure of a surpassing life.

Listen actively this week and experience a new level of effective communication.

Action Points

- ▸ Be an active listener.
- ▸ Remove distractions so you can focus on the person.
- ▸ Take notes.
- ▸ Paraphrase back.
- ▸ Show open body language.
- ▸ Hear both sides.
- ▸ Don't solve the problem unless asked.
- ▸ Document the meeting.

 ## Payoff

Great understanding, more effectiveness, rich relationships!

20. Love Is

*One of the hardest things in this world is to admit
you are wrong. And nothing is more helpful in
resolving a situation than its frank admission.*
— BENJAMIN DISRAELI

*If you don't accept responsibility for your actions, then
you are forever chained to a position of defense.*
— HOLLY LISLE

*A brother wronged is more unyielding than a fortified
city; disputes are like the barred gates of a citadel.*
— BIBLE, PROVERBS 18:19

To err is human, to blame the next guy even more so.
— UNKNOWN

The nine most powerful words in the English language are the least used, and most needed. Because people, especially leaders, don't use these words, relationships are broken and countless hours are wasted defending indefensible positions. The corporate world is filled with "blame avoiders" who attempt to deflect or defend bad choices or poor performance. The higher these avoiders are in an organization, the more damage they do, the more people they harm, and the greater resources they waste attempting to justify their actions. The longer a mistake goes on, the greater the damage. These are straightforward truths. Yet, most people will do anything to prevent admitting a mistake.

When someone has the courage to use these nine words, respect increases and relationships deepen. People who want to live a surpassing life have the confidence to use these words quickly when the need arises, and thus strengthen their bonds with others.

The nine words are: "I was wrong. I am sorry. Please forgive me." Simple and direct, factual and emotional, without rationalization or excuse, these words are the hallmark of strong individuals and leaders.

No one expects perfection or that a leader will never make a mistake. What people can expect is that a person quickly and genuinely admits the mistake, so everyone can move on.

Sadly, leaders are the least likely to confess that they were wrong. Instead, they often demand their staff defend an error with countless analyses and presentations. "We think the merger was a good idea, despite our stock dropping 50 percent. My staff will now show you why." Such leaders are often afraid that admitting a mistake will undermine their credibility, when they are just further damaging their believability by denying their error. It is much better to come clean quickly and spend time determining a corrective course.

Business and personal relationships can benefit greatly from using the nine words. I had a confrontation with an executive at Disney. It was a small matter, but got quickly blown out of proportion, escalating to both of our bosses. I finally made an appointment with the executive at her office. When I arrived and walked in, it was apparent she was "ready for battle." I said, "I was wrong. I am sorry. Will you please forgive me?" She was speechless. All the arguments she had prepared were suddenly moot. She stammered, "Yes, of course." We shared a few more moments of conversation and I left. When I got back to my office, my boss called. "What did you say to her?" he asked incredulously, "Because she is telling everyone what a great person you are!" It's sad that, in the corporate world, admitting you are wrong is such an unusual occurrence that it gets a response like this. I could have maintained my innocence, and we could have continued in battle, wasting precious resources and time. Instead, by my taking responsibility for my actions and admitting my mistake, we were able to move on and build a great relationship.

Contrary to Erich Segal's quote that "love is not ever having to say you are sorry," most spouses would love to hear the nine words. Often, if one spouse is willing to admit his or her mistakes, the other spouse will become comfortable enough to do the same. I expect many divorces could have been avoided if couples used the nine words more often.

As you think about your relationships, who needs to hear an apology from you? Use the nine words, and you will start to build deeper bonds with your loved ones and business partners.

Action Point

Who needs to hear the words "I was wrong. I am sorry. Please forgive me."? Go and talk to that person today.

Payoff

Freedom from guilt, less defensiveness, awesome relationships!

81

21. Stinky Feet

*Never criticize a man until you've walked
a mile in his moccasins.*
— NATIVE AMERICAN PROVERB

Can a man who's warm understand one who's freezing?
— ALEXANDER SOLZHENITSYN

*He who is carried on another's back does not
appreciate how far off the town is.*
— AFRICAN PROVERB

*Think of yourselves the way Christ Jesus thought of
himself. He had equal status with God but didn't think
so much of himself that he had to cling to the advantages
of that status no matter what. Not at all. When the
time came, he set aside the privileges of deity and
took on the status of a slave, became human! Having
become human, he stayed human. It was an incredibly
humbling process. He didn't claim special privileges.*
— BIBLE, PHILIPPIANS 2:5–7

As part of my Disney training, I completed over 400 hours of
"in-costume" training at over fifty different roles and locations
at Walt Disney World. As a Vice President, I hauled trash at
the Magic Kingdom, made beds at the Grand Floridian, sold
tickets at Epcot, cleaned the broiler at quick service restaurants,
and sold merchandise in the stores. This was long before the
popularity of programs like "Undercover Boss."

With each experience, I gained an appreciation for how tough these jobs are. My back ached after making beds for eight hours. I was hot, sweaty and dirty from being a custodian. I understood what it was like to be asked, "Where are the restrooms?" one hundred times a day. I also developed strong relationships with the Cast Members who worked with me. These were the people closest to our guests, and I learned about barriers that prevented our Cast Members from providing outstanding service—issues I was able to fix back in the office. Afterward, I often received calls from people who had worked with me about how new policies were helping or hindering their efforts to provide great service.

Most of the Cast Members were amazed that a VP would come work alongside them. To me, it was not that unusual, as I had the same experience early in my career. In the summer between your first and second years at the Naval Academy, you go to the fleet and serve as an enlisted person. You sleep in the enlisted quarters, dine in the enlisted mess, and perform the same duties as a new enlisted person (which frequently involved cleaning bilges). Before you learn to lead, you need to learn to serve, and this early training was a crucial lesson.

Walking in another's shoes relates to personal and community relationships as well as the work environment. I used to get very annoyed with screaming children on planes until I had my own children and found out that, despite the best efforts at distraction and soothing, it is very difficult to quiet a young child. Now, I try to smile and help, rather than criticize and condemn. Many spouses gain a new appreciation for their partner when left alone with the children for a few days. We all have blind spots and walking in someone else's shoes is a quick way to have our eyes opened.

I helped at a homeless shelter as part of the Lifework Leadership program. I had lunch with a homeless man that was my age and asked him about his story. He described growing up never knowing his father, with a mother who was a drug addict. His neighborhood was violent and depressing, full of crime and drugs. As I listened to him, I wondered if I would have ended up homeless had I been born into his life. I came from a stable, highly intelligent, two-parent family and grew up in the safety of the suburbs. Education was highly valued in my home, with college and even graduate school an expectation. We read newspapers, discussed world events and traveled extensively. All of these advantages are huge benefits that my homeless friend lacked. That experience dramatically changed my perspective on those in need and helped mold my view of generosity and helping others.

Walking in another person's shoes creates empathy, respect, appreciation and humility. We become slower to judge, more compassionate and wiser. We see opportunities more clearly and often create bonds that help us achieve those opportunities. All these benefits are part of a surpassing life and increase the diversity and depth of our relationships.

 Action Points

- Be willing to work alongside others to better understand them.
- If you are in a leadership role, have your staff people work on the front line, especially in busy periods.
- Be careful of your blind spots. If you are particularly judgmental of someone, put yourself in their shoes.

▸ As you consider being generous, think about if you lived in their circumstances.

 Payoff

Compassion, wisdom, respect for others, and humility.

22. Help, I Need Somebody

*The healthy, the strong individual is the one
who asks for help when he needs it. Whether he
has an abscess on his knee or in his soul.*
— RONA BARRETT

*A friend is someone who will help you move. A real
friend is someone who will help you move a body.*
— UNKNOWN

*He comes alongside us when we go through hard times,
and before you know it, he brings us alongside someone
else who is going through hard times so that we can be
there for that person just as God was there for us.*
— BIBLE, 2 CORINTHIANS 1:4

Culturally, Americans have been taught never to ask for help.
Sports superstars and celebrities, and even fictional characters
like the Marlboro Man, James Bond and Tommy Bahama
promulgate the idea of the independent loner who doesn't
need anyone. The media portrays asking for help as weakness
and failure and considers it newsworthy when a public figure
asks for help. Yet, the reality is most people respect those who
recognize their needs and admit they need help. Letting people
know that you don't know something or need help makes you
authentic—a real person. Those who never admit a need are
actually considered fake and insecure.

Leaders are especially prone to denying their weaknesses.
Many carry the perception that they have to show "a stiff upper

lip" or bury any personal feelings for the sake of the business. They practice being emotionless, neither celebratory in positive events nor sad in tough times. When asked if there is anything that can be done for them, they respond with the obligatory, "No, everything is under control. I don't need a thing."

My mother died when I was leading Epcot. There was no question in my mind that I would share that with people. Many would tell me about their own losses of loved ones and how they dealt with death. We immediately created an additional bond and deeper relationship. It would be sad to miss that by keeping my loss a secret.

After 9/11, Cast Members would frequently ask me if they could do anything for me. Everyone saw the attendance decline, and the fear of job loss was palpable. I could have said, "No, there is nothing you can do. We have everything under control," but that would have minimized them and not been truthful. Instead, I told them to "go out there and completely 'love on' every Guest that we do have so they go home and tell all their friends that they have to go to Epcot." I also said, "If you see any ways that we can reduce costs while maintaining great service, let me know, because we need every idea we can get." The Guests that came during that time had a fabulous experience, and they did go home and tell their friends. I also had many front line Cast Members come forward with ideas about how to reduce costs that we were able to implement. Asking for help gets powerful results and builds morale, breaking down walls between people.

If you are asked, "How are you doing?" do you answer the question honestly? I've found a good way to ask that question is to follow it with a 1–10 scale: "How are you doing—1 to 10, with one awful and ten great?" This is particularly good with teenagers or others who are "self-reliant" and typically give you a "Fine, no problems" response. Most people need a little push, and then often give a more honest answer.

Wise people willingly admit their needs in any and all situations. They have enough self-esteem to admit that they don't know everything and can't do it all on their own. They have no problem freely accepting help. Other people can much more easily relate to them and share their own stories of situations when they also asked for help. With surpassing living, asking for help is a sign of strength and builder of healthy relationships.

 Action Points

► Recognize that asking for help is a sign of authenticity, not weakness.
► Celebrate good times and grieve tough situations.
► Be honest with people about the situation, and ask them to rise to the challenge.
► Use the 1–10 scale to find out how people are really doing.
► Freely accept help.

 Payoff

Open, honest relationships, much stronger teams, help in times of need.

CHAPTER 5

Knowledge Beyond Measure

All men by nature desire knowledge.
— ARISTOTLE

To be conscious that you are ignorant
is a great step to knowledge.
— BENJAMIN DISRAELI

If a man empties his purse into his head, no one
can take it away from him. An investment in
knowledge always pays the best interest.
— BENJAMIN FRANKLIN

The heart of the discerning acquires knowledge,
for the ears of the wise seek it out.
— BIBLE, PROVERBS 18:15

KNOWLEDGE CARRIES OVER into all aspects of life. Knowledgeable people tend to be healthier, have larger incomes and net worth, attain honor, and maintain relationships. The knowledge you gain from reading this book will help you in many areas of your life. Attaining knowledge requires action—it is not a passive event. There are smart ways to gain expertise and surpassing people use them to become wise.

23. 130 Million Books

A room without books is like a body without a soul.
— CICERO

The rules have changed. True power is held by the person who possesses the largest bookshelf, not gun cabinet or wallet.
— ANTHONY J. D'ANGELO

If we encounter a man of rare intellect, we should ask him what books he reads.
— RALPH WALDO EMERSON

When my son was in high school, he complained about all the reading he had to do. He said, "Dad, I don't understand why we have to read all these books and memorize facts. If I need to know anything, I can just Google it." He had an excellent point. Unlike the pre-Internet days when you had to look up topics in the encyclopedia or visit the library for information, today almost anything you need to know is available instantly by computer or smartphone. Dinnertime debates about people or facts can be immediately settled with an iPhone. So, why bother to read books any more?

Successful people read books. The amount of time spent reading is directly correlated to academic success and income. If you read more, you will do better in school and earn more money—it is as simple as that.

The conclusion of an extensive National Endowment of the Arts study entitled, *To Read or Not to Read: A Question of National Significance*, is powerful:

All of the data suggest how powerfully reading transforms the lives of individuals—whatever their social circumstances. Regular reading not only boosts the likelihood of an individual's academic and economic success—facts that are not especially surprising—but it also seems to awaken a person's social and civic sense. Reading correlates with almost every measurement of positive personal and social behavior surveyed. It is reassuring, though hardly amazing, that readers attend more concerts and theater than non-readers, but it is surprising that they exercise more and play more sports—no matter what their educational level. The cold statistics confirm something that most readers know but have mostly been reluctant to declare as fact—books change lives for the better.

The study noted that the decline in reading is a serious national problem, highlighting the sobering statistics that:

- Nearly half of all Americans ages eighteen to twenty-four read no books for pleasure.
- Fifteen- to twenty-four-year-olds spend only seven to ten minutes per day on voluntary reading—about 60 percent less time than the average American, while spending two to two and a half hours per day watching TV. This activity consumes the most leisure time for men and women of all ages.
- American families are spending less on books than at almost any other time in the past two decades, even though the number of books in a home is a significant predictor of academic achievement.
- Reading proficiency rates are stagnant or declining in adults of both genders and all education levels.

- Poor reading skills are endemic in the prison population, with 56 percent of adult prisoners reading at or below the Basic level and only 3 percent reading at a Proficient level.

The benefits of reading are shown by these results:

- More than 60 percent of employed Proficient readers have jobs in management, or in the business, financial, professional, and related sectors, compared to only 18 percent of Basic readers employed in those fields.
- Proficient readers are two and a half times as likely as Basic readers to be earning $850 or more a week.
- Literary readers are more than three times as likely as non-readers to visit museums, attend plays or concerts, and create artworks of their own.
- They are also more likely to play sports, attend sporting events, or do outdoor activities. As an example, 72 percent of readers exercise compared to 40 percent for non-readers.

Common excuses for a lack of reading are, "I don't have the time," "I've never been a good reader," "I have a hard time finding a book that interests me." None are valid. The busiest, most successful people find time to read books. They recognize that reading is an investment that pays high returns. "Poor readers" can improve their proficiency by reading, just as those who are out of shape improve with exercise. Saying that you can't find something to read when there are over 130 million books in the world defies belief. There is no good excuse for not reading books.

There are ways, though, to leverage your reading time. For example, I read book summaries provided through services like

Audio-Tech or Soundview. For a minimal cost (typically less than $100 per year), you get two to three book summaries per month. These summaries capture key ideas in the books and take fifteen to thirty minutes to read. If a particular summary interests me, I will buy the book. Otherwise, I have the benefit of much of the thinking for only a few dollars and spend a fraction of the time it would take to read the entire book.

I read three newspapers daily—my local paper, the *Wall Street Journal* and the *New York Times*. Since I don't watch television, this replaces morning and nightly TV news for me.

I also subscribe to a number of daily emails that provide useful, summary information, such as *Harvard Business Review*, *Wired* magazine and my local business newspaper. Google Alerts allow me to get emails when news occurs on specific topics. All of these take seconds to scan, and keep me current.

For leisure reading, I have recently read biographies, particularly of significant leaders. It is fascinating to see how a leader's background prepared him or her for their leadership role, and then put myself in their situation, think about what I would have done, and compare plans. This fundamental approach is the foundation of Harvard Business School's case study method. Students are given a "case," putting them in a specific business situation, and asked what they would do. They then find out what the company leaders did, and the outcome. By "actively reading" and placing yourself in the position of others, you engage in the story and learn much more.

Knowledge is condensed experience, and the best way to get this experience is through reading. Crack open a book today and start living the surpassing life.

Action Points

- ► Read, read, read—no excuses!
- ► Leverage your reading time with book summaries.
- ► Read newspapers instead of watching TV news.
- ► Subscribe to daily emails.
- ► Actively read by putting yourself into the story and determining how you would respond.

Payoff

Greater knowledge, academic success and financial reward, smarter kids, positive personal and social behavior.

24. Ask Questions

Judge a man by his questions rather than by his answers.
— VOLTAIRE

*The real object of education is to have a man in
the condition of continually asking questions.*
— BISHOP CREIGHTON

*Man has made some machines that can answer questions
provided the facts are profusely stored in them, but
we will never be able to make a machine that will
ask questions. The ability to ask the right question is
more than half the battle of finding the answer.*
— THOMAS WATSON

I reported to my submarine after completing four years at the
Naval Academy and another one and a half years of nuclear
power training and submarine school. I figured I had all the
answers, or at least that I was expected to have all the answers.

All submarine officers have to complete qualifications after
they get to their ship. These qualifications are specific to the
ship and require that you learn all the different compartments
and operations. You study the material and are then quizzed
by Chief Petty Officers (CPO) or Officers, like the Engineer
or Navigator, who sign off on your qualifications after you
demonstrate adequate knowledge. After you complete all of
your qualifications (typically a one to two year process), you
are allowed to wear the coveted gold dolphins insignia on your
uniform.

Early in my time onboard, I was working on qualifying in the torpedo room. The CPO in charge of the torpedo room was very proud of his space and his people. He wanted everyone who qualified in his torpedo room to be well versed. I was struggling with his questions and resorted to making up answers, since I was afraid to display my ignorance. To my relief, he seemed to accept my answers and finally signed my book.

Three years later, as I was leaving the ship, I went to the torpedo room CPO to say goodbye. He said, "Lieutenant Rex, I didn't respect you very much when you first came to the ship. You pretended to know more than you did. But, during your time onboard, you learned to admit what you didn't know and ask questions. I respect you for that, and I'm sorry to see you go."

This was a great learning experience for me, although I often forgot the lesson and reverted back to my old behavior when I was put in new situations. Over time, I determined a few reasons why other people (and I) often don't ask questions:

People are afraid to admit that they don't know something that they are supposed to know.

This was my issue on the submarine. I would like to say that, from that point on, I never tried to fake it and I always asked questions, but I can't. I've had to learn over the last twenty years that it is okay to admit what you don't know, and people respect you more, not less, when you ask questions. As a leader, the people who follow you particularly like it when you ask them how they do their job. It reverses the power dynamic, with the employee demonstrating his expertise and value.

They don't have enough knowledge to ask a question.

There are many questions that can be asked in any situation. A great booklet that I have carried and used for years is *Asking to Win!* by Bobb Biehl. Biehl provides questions for a variety of situations, including getting to know someone better, interviewing, brainstorming, decision-making, organizing, planning and parenting. He presents the most powerful question as Why? . . . Why? . . . Why? . . . Why? and the ideal question as "What is the ideal?" I have particularly used his questions in the section on career change to confirm or reject different job opportunities.

Preparation is also crucial in asking good questions. If you are meeting with someone or interviewing at a company, always do your homework and be prepared to ask specific questions. When I have interviewed with executives at a company, I have prepared one-page sheets for each person that I am meeting. The sheets have specific questions related to their area (e.g., finance, operations, marketing) based on the research I have done on the company. The sheet also has several more general questions that I ask everyone (e.g., "What is the one thing that you would do to make the company better?"). This is an efficient way to capture valuable information and keep everything straight after multiple interviews.

They are hoping someone else will ask the question.

Many people won't ask questions due to shyness, laziness, insecurity or pride, and are more than happy to "delegate" that responsibility to others. Some are inhibited by childhood memories of parents telling them to "Stop asking so many questions!" Yet, if you can overcome these fears and inhibitions, you can stand out and be remembered as a person who asks great questions and gains useful knowledge.

Surpassing people practice the art of questioning, combining preparation, boldness and humility in a powerful mix to satisfy their curiosity and attain wisdom.

 Action Points

- ▸ Don't fake it. Admit what you don't know and ask questions.
- ▸ Learn general questions that apply to many situations.
- ▸ Prepare yourself to ask specific questions.
- ▸ Recognize and overcome any anxiety you have about asking questions.

 Payoff

Constant learning, greater knowledge, a reputation of curiosity and boldness.

25. To Thine Own Self Be True

The first principle is that you must not fool yourself—
and you are the easiest person to fool.
— RICHARD FEYNMAN

One must know oneself, if it does not serve to discover truth,
it at least serves as a rule of life, and there is nothing better.
— BLAISE PASCAL

Delusions of grandeur make me feel a lot better about myself.
— JANE WAGNER

One of the most important types of knowledge you need to acquire is self-knowledge. Many people get book knowledge or street smarts, but never get to know their own strengths, passions, blind spots, and weaknesses. This ignorance results in inferior performance and even complete personal failure. Sadly, when failure occurs, the person often looks back and sees the times when they could have gained self-knowledge and deeply regrets the missed opportunities.

I'm an assessment junkie. Over my thirty years in the military and corporate world, I've taken about every test possible. Myers-Briggs, DISC, Gallup Profile, Gallup StrengthsFinder, 360 degree feedback, corporate assessments, health assessments— you name it, and I have probably taken it. This is not because of any love for standardized tests. Rather, it reflects my desire to know as much as possible about myself and my leadership. I have discovered whom I work well with, and whom I need to partner with to make up for my weaknesses. I've found out things that I like to do and excel in, and other things that I need to minimize or delegate. The assessments have helped me to become a better person and leader.

Whenever I do an assessment, I have my wife read the results and tell me whether she thinks it is accurate. Having lived with me for over thirty years, I figure she should have the best picture of who I am and how I behave. Invariably, she will agree with the assessment. It amazes me a test can determine my inner psyche from answering a series of multiple choice questions! As much as I may want to challenge the results, it's hard to refute multiple assessments (and my wife) that all concur on the conclusions.

I think one of the most useful assessments is Gallup StrengthsFinder. This test showed my strengths as Responsibility, Maximizer, Achiever, Learning and Belief. The analyst who discussed the results with me said my profile matched a classic workaholic. "Companies must love you, because your Maximizer means you always want to improve things, your Achiever pushes you to do more and take on new challenges, and your Responsibility means you will get the job done." I felt pretty good about her comments, until she concluded, "Of course, people like you die at an early age from a heart attack." Fortunately, that part of her assessment has not come true, but she did cause me to evaluate my work habits and make worthwhile changes.

We often tend to view others through the lens of our own personality and gravitate toward those who are like us. Being self-aware can ensure that you don't fall into this blind spot, and that you have diverse friends and employees. It also prevents you from being overly critical of people who aren't like you. For example, people who didn't have the strength of Responsibility used to drive me crazy. I viewed them as lazy or disorganized.

After doing the assessments, I recognized that many people do not score as highly in this area as I do, and I need to be much more forgiving.

If you are a leader, you should have your team go through an assessment process, and review the composite results. You will likely find that your team lacks strengths in particular areas, and you should consider this with your next hire.

With the easy availability of inexpensive, on-line assessments, you don't have any excuse when it comes to knowing yourself. Seek self-knowledge, and you will find a surpassing life.

 ## Action Points

- ▸ Take advantage of every opportunity to go through an assessment process and learn more about your strengths, weaknesses, interests and abilities.
- ▸ Check the results with someone who knows you well, like parents, close friends or your spouse. Ask them to make you aware of when you are displaying strengths, weaknesses or blind spots.
- ▸ Use the results of your assessment to change the way you look at others so you are more understanding.
- ▸ Have your team do individual assessments, and then review the composite to determine your team's strengths and weaknesses.

 ## Payoff

Higher individual and team performance, improved interpersonal relationships, not dying young from a heart attack!

26. Thirteen Years

I find television very educating. Every time somebody turns on the set, I go into the other room and read a book.
— GROUCHO MARX

Many people tell me that they are stressed due to lack of time. "I don't have any time to read books." "I'd like to spend more time on relationships and keeping in touch with people, but I'm so busy." "I know I should spend more time with my kids, but I have too much else going on." My response to these concerns is always the same question, "Do you watch TV?"

The average American watches four to six hours of television per day. Assuming you are better than the average, let's say you watch three hours of television per day, or twenty-one hours in a week. If you do the math, you'll find out that, in a six-year period, you will have spent one year of your waking life watching TV! In an eighty-year lifespan, you will have spent **thirteen years** watching television, the equivalent of going to college, law school and medical school.

Think about getting back all those years of your life just by turning off the tube—all the books you could have read, the people you could have contacted, the value to your children of having their parent for additional years, and the physical benefits of having extra years of exercise.[8]

---

[8] A study published in the *Journal of British Sports Medicine* showed that for every hour spent watching television, you reduce your life by twenty-two minutes. This is similar to a lifelong smoker, whose average lifespan reduction is five years. Turn off the tube and you will live a longer, healthier life.

My children also did not watch television when they were growing up. When he was in elementary school, my son came to me one day and asked, "If I don't watch TV, will you pay me?" I looked at him quizzically, and he pointed to a newspaper article about a boy who asked his dad the same question. The dad agreed to pay him, but only if he went for an entire year without watching any television. The boy did it, and both father and son were happy with the result. I thought it was a great idea and immediately said "Yes."

We drew up a contract that specified the payment and any exceptions (such as watching pre-approved coverage like historical events and the Superbowl; watching TV on vacation or a friend's house if they are watching it, etc.). My son and twin daughters all agreed and signed the contract.

During that year, instead of watching TV, the kids read, played outside, put on shows and participated in sports. There were a few times when they missed television, especially when friends were talking about specific shows. But, they quickly got into new habits that didn't center on the tube.

At the end of the year, we congratulated them for going an entire year without watching television, and paid them as we had agreed. I asked them if they wanted to do it again, got a resounding "No," and the TV returned.

About two weeks later, the kids came back to Nancy and me wanting to do TV-free again. When I asked them why they had changed their mind, they said: "We fight over what to watch." "The programs are really stupid." "We'd rather get the money." One of my daughters, Monica, had a classic statement: "If you don't watch it, you don't miss it." As you watch television, you realize that many of the ads are designed to get you to keep watching: "Don't miss the next episode of _____."

"The new season starts next week. Be sure to see the amazing premiere." If you aren't exposed to these teasers, you are much less motivated to "tune in next week."

They signed their new contracts and peace reigned in the house once more. We also noticed another phenomenon. When we asked the kids what they wanted for birthdays or Christmas, they had a hard time coming up with ideas. When they had watched TV, they usually wanted the "hot toy" that was heavily marketed. Without this influence, marketers no longer manipulated their desires. They were also not exposed to the violence, sexuality, negativity and addictive behaviors frequently portrayed in television shows.

My children are all exceptional students and thoughtful adults. When I asked them what they believe made a difference, they responded that refusing to watch television was the best decision they had made while growing up. For a surpassing life, go cold turkey and turn off the tube. It may be the best decision of your life.

 Action Points

> ▸ Go cold turkey and turn off the tube!
> ▸ If you have children, do a TV-free contract.
> ▸ Use your new time to read books, renew relations, write, exercise or do volunteer work.

 Payoff

A healthier, smarter, and more satisfying life.

CHAPTER 6
Leadership Beyond Measure

A leader is a dealer in hope.
— NAPOLEON BONAPARTE

If your actions inspire others to dream more, learn more, do more and become more, you are a leader.
— JOHN QUINCY ADAMS

Whatever Saul gave David to do, he did it—and did it well. Everybody, both the people in general and Saul's servants, approved of and admired David's leadership.
— BIBLE, 1 SAMUEL 18:5

DO YOU WANT TO BE A GOOD LEADER? I hope not. You should aspire to be a great leader. There is a huge difference between good and great leaders. Think about a great leader you have worked for. It might have been a business leader or coach or non-profit leader. You enjoyed working for this person and grew under his or her leadership. All aspects of your life were better, and you looked forward to getting up every day. To this day, you probably model behaviors you learned from this leader, so, although you no longer work for him, his leadership still impacts people.

I want you to be not only a great leader, but in the top one percent of all leaders. This is surpassing leadership. If you Google the word "leadership," you will get over 400 million hits. Most articles and writings discuss how to improve your leadership or become a "great" leader. Very few, though, describe how to become a top 1 percent leader. Surpassing leaders are in this rare group.

The previous sections provided a foundation for surpassing living. This section extends surpassing thinking specifically for leaders, to maximize their effectiveness.

27.   Eagle Eyes

Like the horizons for breadth and the ocean for depth,
the understanding of a good leader is broad and deep.
— BIBLE, PROVERBS 25:3

An eagle's eyes are at least four times sharper than a human. This allows an eagle to see a rabbit from a mile in the air, and swoop down for an afternoon treat. The eagle cannot only see much farther than a human; it can also discern opportunities, diving down to take advantage of them. Leaders need to have similar vision—seeing opportunities from further away and then capturing them quickly.

I'm frequently asked to define the ideal leader. My consistent response is "a strategic thinker and tactical implementer." In your leadership, you should aspire to acquire these two capabilities or, if you lack one, to partner with someone who can complement you.

In his book, *Visionary Leadership*, Burt Nanus defines a vision as "a realistic, credible, attractive future for your organization. It is your articulation of a destination toward which your organization should aim, a future that is better, more successful, or more desirable of your organization than is the present."[9] Nanus contends that the right vision "is an idea so energizing that it in effect jump-starts the future by calling forth the skills, talents, and resources to make it happen."[10] There are tremendous strategic thinkers who can develop visions as described by Nanus. Often though, these thinkers cannot

9   Burt Nanus, *Visionary Leadership*, page 8
10   *Ibid.*, page 9

successfully implement their visions, and they either remain dreams or frustrating failures.

On the other hand, there are some great tacticians and managers who can ensure a plan is executed—they just can't develop one. They lack a "big picture" perspective, and often prefer to maintain and optimize the current operation rather than step out into new territory. Their companies often fail to grow and sometimes fail completely.

When I led Epcot, I developed a vision for the park which led to a four-point strategy. Using that strategy, we developed a multi-year tactical plan, with prioritized objectives for each year. Everyone knew the vision, strategy and specific tactics for their area, and we could measure our progress on a regular basis. It was amazing to see the ideas that were generated by the leaders and front-line Cast Members once they knew the vision and strategy.

The surpassing leader is able to fly at a high level, envisioning where the organization is today and where it can be in the future. She sees the potential barriers and charts a path around them. Then, she is able to translate the vision into a tactical plan, and ensure the tactical plan is followed. When necessary, she can easily change from the 30,000-foot level and swoop down into the details as a problem arises. Her company, employees and community benefit from this ideal leader.

 Action Points

> ► Are you a strategic thinker and tactical implementer?
> ► If you lack ability in one of the two areas, either work on building it up or partner with someone who can help you.

- What is your vision for your organization?
- Have you created a multi-year, prioritized tactical plan to bring your vision to fruition?
- Have you shared your vision and plan throughout your organization and asked for implementation ideas, especially from your front line employees?

 ## Payoff

Leadership success, organizational alignment, leaving competitors in the dust.

28. Sick of Your Own Voice

Any idea, plan or purpose may be placed in
the mind through repetition of thought.
— Napoleon Hill

Sent does not mean received.
— Tom Sachs

"I sent out a memo. Why didn't anyone respond?" "We had a town hall and shared the new strategy, but when I ask someone about it, they acted like they never heard it." "We posted our monthly focus, but no one seems to have changed their behavior." Many leaders have had these and similar experiences, as I did early in my career. You think you have communicated an important idea, but no one seems to be listening.

Amidst this frustration, I had an "aha" moment when I read an article on human behavior. The article stated that a person has to hear or see a message seven times before taking action on it, and then the message has to be repeated every twenty-eight days to keep the behavior going. Did you ever wonder why you hear the same ads over and over again? It is because marketers know you won't respond if you hear it just once. There is some debate over the number of times you need to hear a message (some researchers claim as high as twenty times), but there is a consensus around the concept of effective frequency—the optimal number of times that you need to be exposed before you act.

As a leader, you need to plan to share your messages multiple times in multiple ways if you want a response. You must take every opportunity to communicate your vision, strategy and specific tactics. When you reach the point that you are sick and tired of the repetition and believe that everyone has the message, your people will just be starting to get it. This is not because they are unintelligent or apathetic—it is the nature of human behavior and brain chemistry.

The need for repetition has significant implications:

1. Your message has to be simple. When I led our diversity and inclusion efforts at Epcot, our rallying cries were to build a "Home for Diversity" and to be "Radically Inclusive." These short phrases were easy to remember, emotionally satisfying and highly repeatable. Similarly, when I went to Hilton Grand Vacations, I told our Team Members that we wanted to create "Hilton Grand Lifetime Fans." Contrast these phrases with the lengthy diversity statements or customer satisfaction goals presented at some companies that no one remembers or acts upon.

2. You must create a communication plan that provides constant repetition in multiple formats. Some people learn best by reading, others with pictures, audio or video. Short, funny videos are very effective. Think about television commercials that are designed to be memorable and cause an action. Your internal marketing messages should be similar.

3. You must plan to keep your message for a long time. Leaders are taught that "change is good," and so they change visions and strategies frequently—often when they are bored with the current plan. Unfortunately, because of the repetition required to create change, the front line is often just starting to get it and change behavior when the strategy is changed. This causes the familiar "flavor of the

month" lament and disengaged team members. The larger the organization, the longer you need to keep a consistent message, so think about it carefully before you roll it out.

4. Leaders throughout the organization should share the script. The CEO and executive team need to lead the way, but cannot be the sole source. Team Members want to hear directly from their leaders, and see that their leaders have embraced and acted upon the message.

5. Creativity is key, and the best creations come from the front line. Engage your front line Team Members in sharing ways to get the message across. The best way to do this is through competitions. We had a flag competition around diversity with our teams at Epcot, and then displayed the flags at our annual picnic so everyone could vote. The flags were incredibly creative, the teams had fun doing them, and the message about diversity was embraced.

When you get frustrated about the lack of response, remember that it is not due to your lack of communication skills, but rather the need to repeat the same message multiple times.

 Action Points

- ▶ Expect that you will need to repeat your message many, many times before it becomes part of the culture.
- ▶ Keep it short.
- ▶ Use multiple formats.
- ▶ Plan to keep the same message for multiple years if you want it to sink in.
- ▶ Employees want to hear the message from their direct leader.

▶ Leverage your employees' creativity to get a message across.

 Payoff

Effective communication, desired behavior, organizational success.

29. Uniform Races

There is never enough time, unless you're serving it.
— MALCOLM FORBES

*He who every morning plans the transactions of the day
and follows out that plan, carries a thread that will guide
him through the maze of the most busy life. But where
no plan is laid, where the disposal of time is surrendered
merely to the chance of incidence, chaos will soon reign.*
— VICTOR HUGO

All my possessions for a moment of time.
— ELIZABETH I

*How does a project get to be a year behind
schedule? One day at a time.*
— FRED BROOKS

Besides active listening, the second most important skill for
successful leaders is time management. A common refrain
heard when talking about great leaders is "how do they manage to do it all?" The secret is effectively using every minute of
every day. There are 525,600 minutes in a year. How well do
you use each one?

I learned the value of a minute at the Naval Academy during my first year (Plebe) summer. Plebe summer is an intense
training period when you are indoctrinated into the military
way of life. During the two months, you are purposefully
required to do much more than can be physically done in the

time allotted. One of the favorite exercises during the summer is "uniform races." All the plebes are lined up in the hall. An upperclassman yells out a uniform and a time ("Dress Whites. Two minutes. Go."). You are required to race back to your room, change into that uniform, and return within the specified time. Sometimes, you are required to take a shower or shave in between changing. Other times, you will be given instructions to put on different combinations of uniforms. For the first few uniform races, very few plebes make it back in time. But, as the summer progresses, you learn how to optimize and shave seconds off each step in the process. You start off thinking that you could never change in two minutes, and end up finding out that you can do it with time to spare. You find out just how much you can do in two minutes. I learned the value of uniform races when the academic year started, and I had to change clothes quickly during the day. I also saw the value when I entered the business world, and often had to race from a late business meeting or flight and change clothes for dinner.

The best use of your time is to take a great time management course. Lee Cockerell, former EVP of Operations for Walt Disney World, teaches a comprehensive and highly effective time management program. Lee is so passionate about time management that he taught the course to thousands of Cast Members when he was at Disney, and continues to teach the course to business leaders today. I encourage every leader to take this course (www.leecockerell.com).

A few of my learnings regarding time management are:

> Write down your tasks. The strongest mind is no match for the weakest pen and paper. My to-do lists when I led Epcot often had over 150 items. There is no way I could ever

remember that many things. By writing them down, I could ensure that nothing slipped through the cracks.

- Prioritize, prioritize, prioritize. Some people use an "A, B, C" system, while others use different symbols or time periods. No matter what you use, you have to make decisions about what needs to be done first.

- Review your items first thing in the morning and last thing in the evening. This gives you a plan for the day, and then feedback about how well you executed on your plan.

- Delegate and "automate." I'll talk about delegation in a later section. For "automate," I am referring to creating habits for the things you do daily. For example, you shouldn't have to think about working out or where you fit it in your calendar. You should have a daily habit of exercising at a particular time and just do it then. Your exercise time might be 6:30–7:30 AM every day. It is in your calendar that way, and you know that is when you work out. Morning and evening routines are not boring—they are a great way to simplify your life.

- Schedule time for the "important" as well as the "urgent." Oftentimes, urgent items crowd out important items, when the important items are more critical to your long-term career. You should classify tasks into Urgent-Important; Not Urgent-Important; Urgent-Not Important; and, Not Urgent-Not Important. Clearly, the Urgent-Important tasks should have a high priority, while Not Urgent-Not Important tasks can most likely be delegated or not even done.

- Schedule thought and "blank" time. Leaders need thought time to develop strategies and process plans. You also need blank time to take care of the urgent items. One of my leaders, Eddie Carpenter, who was the Chief Financial Officer for Disney Parks and Resorts, would typically schedule the day before and the day after his vacations without any meetings. This allowed him to get everything accomplished before he left, and have a day to catch up when he returned, greatly reducing his stress and increasing his productivity.

► Be ruthless about getting rid of non-productive time. Always have something to read or do with you. With smartphones, you can answer emails, read newspapers and make calls using your handheld device. Time is money, and work time is time that you could be spending with your family. Imagine that you are a lawyer that bills $500 per hour—over $8 per minute. Spending twenty minutes in an examining room waiting for a doctor would cost you $160. Don't read old magazines—spend your time on your smartphone doing productive work.

► One of the best pieces of advice from Lee's course is to "do something today that will benefit you in five years." Many people get so caught up in the moment that they don't do anything that will help them in the future. This might include taking care of your health, rebalancing your investment port-folio or contacting someone you haven't talked to in awhile.

John Lithgow said, "Time sneaks up on you like a windshield on a bug." His statement is both humorous and accurate. You need to take control of your time or risk getting squashed by life.

 ## Action Points

► Recognize the value of time. A minute is a long time if you use it well.
► Take a time management course and use either a paper planner or smartphone software to plan your day.

- ▶ Prioritize and review.
- ▶ Delegate and automate.
- ▶ Use waiting time effectively.
- ▶ Do something today that will not benefit you for five to ten years.

 Payoff

A full, rich, rewarding life with accomplishments beyond measure.

30. Ten Cents and a Handkerchief

I will prepare and some day my chance will come.
— ABRAHAM LINCOLN

*It's not the will to win that matters . . . everyone has
that. It's the will to prepare to win that matters.*
— PAUL "BEAR" BRYANT

The time to repair the roof is when the sun is shining.
— JOHN F. KENNEDY

*For we are God's handiwork, created in Christ Jesus to do
good works, which God prepared in advance for us to do.*
— BIBLE, EPHESIANS 2:10

As a Boy Scout, I was taught early in life to "Be Prepared." At
our weekly meetings, we were required to present ten cents
and a handkerchief. The dime was so that we could make an
emergency phone call at a phone booth (yes, it only cost ten
cents to make a call back then and we still had pay phones).
The handkerchief was for emergency first aid, to stop bleeding
or use to tie a splint. More than forty years later, I still carry a
handkerchief in my back pocket and my cell phone is never far
away. Who knows when I might be a first responder at an accident and save someone's life with my compress and phone call?

A huge part of leadership is preparation. Sadly, many of
today's leaders are unprepared. Coaches and business executives
frequently use the phrase "failure to prepare is preparing to

fail." Organizations fail because their leaders are inadequately prepared and don't prepare their employees for the future.

Surpassing leaders are constantly preparing themselves and their teams for new adventures and challenges. These leaders "do their homework," making sure they are knowledgeable about people, companies and their industry. Oftentimes, this comes from reaching out to their friends to get the full story and illustrating the importance of strong relationships. They also manage their time well, preventing the frequent excuse of: "I can barely keep up with the present, much less prepare for the future." They lead in the present while preparing for the future.

Highly successful leaders are usually good negotiators because they are well prepared. Prior to any negotiation, a leader has to spend days and sometimes weeks to ensure he or she is fully prepared. I trained under one of the best negotiators at Disney, Frank Ioppolo. He took our team away for several all-day sessions where we role-played multiple scenarios of point and counterpoint. We thought about every negotiation item, anticipating what the counterparty would ask for and how we would respond. We determined our "walk away" position and how we might reengage the negotiation if we did walk away. It was an extensive, exhausting process. But, when we finally went into the negotiation, we were fully prepared and got a great deal because of Frank's leadership. Through great preparation, we won the battle before it was fought.

Great leaders run great meetings. Effective meeting leaders know that they should spend three to six times the length of the meeting in preparation time. For a one-hour meeting, they would spend three to six hours preparing. I have attended thousands of meetings in my life, and it became apparent very quickly in any meeting when the meeting leader was not well prepared.

Many times someone would call a meeting to discuss a topic. Everyone would show up, gab for a while, and then decide to have another meeting—a waste of time and money. Effective leaders would first ensure a topic required a meeting as opposed to a call or email discussion. They would then prepare a detailed agenda with topics, time for each topic and the person responsible for presenting. In creating the agenda, they might make calls to participants to ensure full knowledge and accountability. A presentation was often sent out in advance for the participants to review and consider. The day before, the meeting would be confirmed with an email and any new information. All actions and decisions were summarized at the end of the meeting, and a confirmation note sent out to all participants. These meetings were highly productive, with great discussions and decision-making. Preparation made all the difference.

To excel beyond measure requires you to prepare beyond measure, or at least more than most good leaders. Your level of preparation determines the level of your leadership. What are you doing today to prepare for your next assignment?

 ## Action Points

- ▸ Do your homework.
- ▸ Prepare for negotiations extensively, using role playing and multiple scenarios.
- ▸ Spend three to six times the length of a planned meeting in preparation time.
- ▸ Always send a detailed agenda and preferably the presentation in advance.
- ▸ Summarize meetings with a follow-up email that includes action items and due dates.

- ▸ Set aside time in your week to prepare for the future.
- ▸ Carry a handkerchief and your cell phone!

 Payoff

Faster career advancement, financial success, greater confidence in all situations.

31. Decisions, Decisions

An executive is a person who always decides; sometimes
he decides correctly, but he always decides.
— JOHN H. PATTERSON

Destiny is a name often given in retrospect to
choices that had dramatic consequences.
— J.K. ROWLING

You have brains in your head.
You have feet in your shoes.
You can steer yourself
any direction you choose.
You're on your own.
And you know what you know.
And YOU are the one who'll decide where to go . . .
— DR. SEUSS

Nothing is more difficult, and therefore more
precious, than to be able to decide.
— NAPOLEON I

Leaders make decisions. The quality of those decisions determines the effectiveness of the leader and the organization. Given the importance of making great decisions, how can a leader enhance the quality of his or her decisions?

Over the years, I've refined my decision-making process, and suggest that you may want to apply many of these same steps when you have to make important decisions.

First, determine the amount of time you have to make a decision. In the event of a casualty situation, decision-making time may be extremely short, and therefore you need to act quickly on limited information. If your house is on fire, it's a quick and easy decision to immediately call 911. When I faced engineering drills on a nuclear submarine or led Epcot on 9/11, I had to make immediate choices. You gather as much information as fast as you can, and then rely on your experience and training to make the best decision possible.

Often, though, people are pressured into making hasty decisions by artificial deadlines. "If you don't buy this house/car/ boat today, it will be gone, and you never get as good a deal!" Salespeople and marketers attempt to create urgency, which often leads to poor decisions: "Limited time deal!" "Order in the next five minutes and get a 20 percent discount!" When I've been pressured for an "immediate answer," I simply say "If you want an answer immediately, then the answer is No."[11] You then typically find out that there was no real immediacy, and you can agree on a more reasonable time frame. Don't be pressured into making a decision before you feel comfortable with the decision and potential outcome.

A second key factor is the importance of a decision. If a choice has minimal impact, make it quickly based on your experience—don't agonize over it. For example, you don't need to go through an extensive decision-making process to pick up a pack of gum at the grocery story, but you might want to complete a thorough evaluation before you purchase a large screen television.

---

[11] This is a particularly helpful phrase if you are parenting teenagers!

You can also remove the need to make many smaller decisions by standardizing your routine. You won't have to "decide" to exercise every day if you have planned for it in your daily routine.

Assuming you have time to make a decision, and the decision has significance, then you should go through a decision-making process. The process should start with correctly framing the question, ensuring that you know what you are trying to decide. This often leads to probing that uncovers a more core issue. You may think the question is, "Should I buy this specific house?" when a better question might be "What is the wisest way to provide a home for my family?" Failure to ask the right question can lead to seriously flawed decisions.

Next, review the information you have and what further information may be useful. You may need to do research, read reviews, ask experts or perform analytics. While more information is generally better, you should determine if the cost and time of acquiring the information justifies its value in the decision-making process. This is an important step, as some people just ask for more data that delays decision-making and increases cost when the additional information has little value. Prioritize your information needs and spend the time and money acquiring the information that has the highest benefit.

Decide who else may be impacted by your decision, and ensure they are informed and have an opportunity to provide input. Operating in isolation risks harming your relationships and can hamper implementing the decision by creating resistance.

If this is a business decision that your leader is interested in, meet with him or her to discuss it and get their point of view. You should also meet with your team or advisors to review the question and information to seek their input and brainstorm ideas, urging "constructive conflict" and open debate. List alternatives and pros/cons. Seek consensus, primarily listening and soliciting dialogue, without necessarily expressing your point of view. If consensus is not possible, after you believe all points had been made, make the decision and explain your rationale.

Try to find a way to say "yes" to new opportunities and push yourself and your team to figure how to do something, rather than figure out the reasons not to do it.

Determine the action plan around the decision, with timetable and accountabilities. Then, ensure the decision, rationale, action plan, timetable and accountabilities are documented and interested parties are informed.

If new information becomes available, be willing to revisit your decision to ensure it is still correct and modify your plans accordingly.

Although taking all these steps will not guarantee a perfect outcome, you will have increased the probability of success. Life is a series of decisions, and, by raising the odds, you improve the likelihood of having a great, surpassing life.

 ## Action Points

- ▸ Make sure you have a sound decision-making process— don't decide important issues on a whim.
- ▸ If a decision is urgent or not very significant, go with your experience, not an extensive process.
- ▸ Don't fall prey to an artificial deadline. You can usually negotiate the time you need to make a good decision.
- ▸ Make sure you are asking the right question before seeking the solution.

- Get input from your advisors and team, and especially those who will be impacted by your decision.
- Have a good debate, then decide and capture your decision on paper.
- Revisit your decision if you get new, substantial information.

 Payoff

Sound decisions, more effective plans, stronger buy-in, easier implementation.

32. Hitting the Beach

*The next day Moses took his place to judge the people.
People were standing before him all day long, from
morning to night. When Moses' father-in-law saw all
that he was doing for the people, he said, "What's going
on here? Why are you doing all this, and all by yourself,
letting everybody line up before you from morning to
night?" Moses said to his father-in-law, "Because the
people come to me with questions about God. When
something comes up, they come to me. I judge between
a man and his neighbor and teach them God's laws and
instructions."*

*Moses' father-in-law said, "This is no way to go
about it. You'll burn out, and the people right along
with you. This is way too much for you—you can't do
this alone. Now listen to me. Let me tell you how to do
this so that God will be in this with you. Be there for
the people before God, but let the matters of concern
be presented to God. Your job is to teach them the rules
and instructions, to show them how to live, what to do.
And then you need to keep a sharp eye out for competent
men—men who fear God, men of integrity, men who
are incorruptible—and appoint them as leaders over
groups organized by the thousand, by the hundred, by
fifty, and by ten. They'll be responsible for the everyday
work of judging among the people. They'll bring the
hard cases to you, but in the routine cases they'll be the
judges. They will share your load and that will make it
easier for you. If you handle the work this way, you'll*

have the strength to carry out whatever God commands
you, and the people in their settings will flourish also."
Moses listened to the counsel of his father-in-law
and did everything he said.
— BIBLE, EXODUS 18:13–24

Even back in Biblical times, leaders had far more to do than they could accomplish by themselves. This fascinating interchange between Moses and his father-in-law shows how Moses was able to successfully lead two million people for over forty years while wandering in the desert. If it worked for Moses, shouldn't it work for you?

Unfortunately, many leaders are fearful of delegation. This limits their growth opportunities, creates a crushing workload, and prevents their people from learning new skills that lead to a stronger bench. Without successful delegation, you will have a poor and much less productive life as a leader.

I learned about delegation early in my career. I had been assigned as the officer in charge of Auxiliary Division. A-Div was responsible for all the non-nuclear engineering on the submarine, such as the hydraulics, compressed air, sanitary, and diesel engine components. The ship was in refit period, which is thirty days between patrols to repair and replenish the ship. We were in the last few days of refit, which was the busiest time. Being a new division officer, I wanted to impress my men by actively participating in the work. We were repairing the diesel generator and I was up to my elbows in grease. I looked up and saw my Chief Petty Officer in civilian clothes with some of the other chiefs. In disbelief, I asked him, "Where do you think you are going?" He stared at me and said, "I'm going to the beach, sir. I figure if you are going to do my job for me, we don't need both of us on the boat."

My chief had given me an early and important lesson about delegating authority and trusting the people who worked for me. From that point on, he was the hands-on leader, and I ended up primarily doing the paperwork.

The key to successful delegation is to ask the question, "Do I absolutely have to do this task, or can someone else do it?" Any time a piece of paper, email, phone call or task crosses my desk, I ask this question. Many leaders rationalize doing tasks themselves with justifications like, "I could give this to someone else, but I can do it faster myself" or "It would take much longer to train someone to do this, so I'll do it this time." These statements are true—in the short run. But, once you do a task yourself, you are destined to continue doing the task from then on. If you add up all the times you might end up doing the task, it is almost always better to spend upfront time delegating, training and following up.

Some leaders feel they have been "burned" by delegating. They delegated a task and it was either not done, or done incorrectly, and impacted their reputation. The phrase that "you can delegate authority, but not responsibility," is correct. Great leaders never use the excuse "I told 'Bob' to do it and he didn't, so it is Bob's fault." When my subordinates would try to blame things on their assistant, my response was "Who does your assistant work for? And, if you can't manage your assistant, how can I be confident you can manage the rest of your team?" When you delegate a task, you have to have a follow-up system. A "tickle" file can be very useful. In a tickle file, you assign a follow-up ("tickle") date to the task, normally a few days to a week before the deadline. The person assigned the task is responsible for letting you know the status by the tickle date. You (or preferably your assistant) keeps track, and, if you don't get a status, you ask for one (with a pointed reminder that you shouldn't have to ask). The tickle file can be paper, with the tickle items filed by date, or electronic, using the Task function in Outlook or Gmail. I had task lists for each of my direct reports, and would review them during our weekly one-on-one sessions. I could get a status on each item and answer any questions, and then we could prioritize the tasks to ensure a reasonable, achievable workload. This way, there were no surprises, and we could reset due dates if necessary.

Delegation doesn't stop with tasks. Whenever I was on vacation, I would delegate my authority to one of my direct reports, rotating through my executives. The Food & Beverage General Manager at Epcot "became" the VP in my absence, with full authority to make decisions. I learned this from assignment to London with British Petroleum. Executives, even at very senior levels, would take long vacations of three to five weeks, going to locales without phones or faxes, leaving a subordinate in charge. When I asked the Treasurer of BP about this as he was preparing to go on vacation, he told me he did it on purpose. "If I left for a week, my people could put off all the decisions until I came back. When it gets to two weeks or more without phone contact, they have to make decisions themselves. This builds their confidence and develops stronger leaders."

This delegation strategy was tested when Nancy and I went to the mountains of North Carolina during one summer when I led Epcot. Cell phone coverage was non-existent. We were having a relaxing, wonderful trip, when we returned to our room after dinner and the message light was blinking. As I picked up the receiver, I hoped the message was from the front desk and not from work. Unfortunately, it was the leader that I had left in charge of Epcot with the terrible news that a four year old boy had died on our Mission: SPACE attraction. As I called him for all the details, my immediate thought was to call off the vacation and return to Epcot. However, he gave me the confidence that he had the situation under control. I also thought that being in charge in a crisis could be a major boost to his development as a leader. I had significant crisis leadership experience from the Navy, 9/11 and other events, and he could benefit from this much more than me. The other leaders on the team would also have to step up and support him in my absence. Primarily for his benefit, I decided to stay on vacation, even though it was incredibly hard to be at the fitness center watching Epcot all over the TV screens wishing I was there. When I returned, he thanked me for the trust I had shown him, and I was very gratified a few years later to see him promoted to a major Vice President position.

Successful delegation frees you and your organization to do far more than you could imagine and exceed beyond expectations.

 ## Action Points

- For every task, ask yourself, "Do I absolutely have to do this or can someone else do it?"
- Don't rationalize doing everything yourself.
- Create a follow-up system to ensure delegated work is completed.

▶ Give your people the opportunity to do your role while you are gone, and give them the freedom to make decisions.

 ## Payoff

Personal success, high morale, strong and capable successors.

33.   This, Too, Shall Pass

An idealist believes the short run doesn't count. A cynic
believes the long run doesn't matter. A realist believes that what
is done or left undone in the short run determines the long run.
— SYDNEY J. HARRIS

In order to be a realist you must believe in miracles.
— HENRY CHRISTOPHER BAILEY

The leader has to be practical and a realist, yet must
talk the language of the visionary and idealist.
— ERIC HOFFER

Suppose one of you wants to build a tower. Won't
you first sit down and estimate the cost to see if
you have enough money to complete it?
— BIBLE, LUKE 14:28

By nature, optimism has to be the default mode for any great
leader. A top leader envisions a better future and shares it with
her followers. No one will follow a leader who promises, "With
my leadership, things will get much worse." While some leaders
are put into a position of admitting a situation will get worse in
the short term, they will quickly add that, after the short term
pain, there will be a much brighter future.

Yet, many leaders take optimism to an extreme. They
want to believe in themselves, their teams and their organizations so much that they presume ultimate success, no matter
what the obstacles. They may be blind to the power of their

competitors; believe that the economy will continue to grow forever; expect that their technology is so superior no one can leapfrog them; price their products too high; tell their customers what they should buy rather than listen to what they want to buy; or, refuse to consider alternative strategies. When it comes to people, overly optimistic people may hire someone who is not that excited to join the organization, thinking "I can change them and get them excited." Or, they may hold on to a poor performer too long, expecting that "I can turn the person around."

What happens when an overly optimistic leader leads an organization? During good times, massive growth plans are developed and implemented, substantially increasing risk. When bad times hit, corrective actions are delayed as the leader can't shift out of his optimism. When the situation finally demands action, the organization has to go through gut-wrenching changes, often overreacting late in the down cycle, and being unprepared for an upturn.

Non-profit organizations are particularly prone to overly optimistic leaders and expectations. Having served on a number of non-profit Boards and worked closely with non-profit leaders, I can attest that non-profit leadership is the most challenging leadership in the world. Non-profits don't have the money, resources, incentives, bonuses and infrastructure of for-profit companies.[12] Non-profits depend primarily on presenting a very

---

[12] Just to clarify, I am speaking here about non-profit organizations, such as charitable or service providers, that don't have revenue and depend on donations, as opposed to "not for profit" businesses like hospitals and universities that have substantial revenue streams and profits. A not-for-profit business can often offer as much or more than a for-profit business since they don't have to pay taxes and get much of their capital at no cost through donations.

compelling vision and an extremely optimistic outlook about the organization's impact. This mindset often carries through the entire non-profit organization and can particularly infect financial projections. Massive building campaigns take place under the assumption attendance will grow and donors will make good on pledges. Leaders hire more and higher-level staff counting on donations to increase. When the expected growth fails to occur, many non-profits either go bankrupt or have to substantially downsize their operations and impact.

Top one percent or surpassing leaders are "realistic optimists." They absolutely believe in their people and organizations and the ability to make a difference in society. They project growth and a brighter future. But, they also understand business cycles, and the need to plan counter cyclically. During boom times, they don't overexpand. They pay down debt and build a cash reserve. They bring on temporary workers and move slowly when adding new buildings and equipment, ensuring that they have sustainable market demand. They maintain discipline in hiring headquarters staff, outsourcing work where possible to keep costs more variable. When lean times come, they reduce their variable costs without impacting customer service. They may expand then, taking advantage of lower construction and equipment costs. They focus on capturing market share, while their competitors struggle. And, when the boom times return, they take a preeminent position in their industry.

A key phrase that captures the thought process of a realistic optimist is "This, too, shall pass." Attributed to a Persian poet, Attar of Nishapur, and quoted by Lincoln, the phrase describes a universal truth about all situations: Neither good times nor bad times last forever. During good times, the realistic optimist enjoys the benefits, but recognizes the cycle will change, and prepares accordingly. During challenging times, she encourages her followers with the assurance that things will get better and prepares for the upswing.

With this balanced, thoughtful approach, the surpassing leader sets herself and her organization apart from the rash optimist or the demoralizing pessimist.

 ## Action Points

- ▸ On a scale of Most Pessimistic to Most Optimistic, where do you typically rank?
- ▸ Do your followers accuse you of being too optimistic? Do you demonstrate any of the behaviors of a leader who is unrealistically optimistic?
- ▸ Where are you in your business cycle today? Have you overreacted, either positively or negatively, to your current situation?
- ▸ Who can you talk to that will help ensure you are being a realistic optimist?

 ## Payoff

Being fully prepared for both ups and downs, leading steadily in all situations.

34. Windows and Mirrors

But those who exalt themselves will be humbled, and
those who humble themselves will be exalted.
— BIBLE, MATTHEW 23:12

Conventional wisdom would tell you to "blow your own horn" to get recognized and advance. However, this negates the importance of surrounding yourself with great people who will be the true drivers of your career. Great people want to work for someone who gives them the credit, rather than keeping the honors and minimizing their contribution.

Jim Collins, in his analysis of the highest levels of leadership in *Good to Great* writes: {*Level 5 Leaders*} *look out the window, not in the mirror, to apportion credit for the success of the company—to other people, external factors, and good luck. {They} look in the mirror, not out the window, to apportion responsibility for poor results, never blaming other people, external factors, or bad luck.* (page 36)

Leaders who are "windows" are secure in their leadership, and don't need to draw attention to their performance. They happily share credit and highlight their people, as they know this credit sharing has two major benefits—it motivates the team to achieve even higher performance and it builds loyalty for the leader. These benefits far outweigh a brief time in the spotlight for the boastful alternative.

These leaders are also "mirrors" who accept responsibility for failures. They earn their pay and title by shielding their teams from corporate wrath. This instills further loyalty as people realize "success has many parents, but failure is an orphan." The focus of the team becomes course correction rather than blame shifting. The team also learns to take risks, knowing the leader "has their back" if the risk doesn't succeed. Most companies say they want to be innovative and take risks, but to do so successfully, they need leaders who accept rather than punish failure.

The best leaders extensively recognize the contributions of their people at all levels. This reinforces positive behaviors and creates strong loyalty. Shortly after Meg Crofton was named as the President of Walt Disney World, she walked Epcot with me. One of the front line Cast Members approached us and I introduced her to Meg. She said, "I was at the movies the other day and thought about Brad." I asked her if it was because of my resemblance to Brad Pitt, and she politely answered, "Not exactly." She went on to say that a few months before, I had witnessed her giving great Guest service, thanked her and gave her a note from me with two movie ticket vouchers in recognition of her work. "No one ever did anything like that for me before," she said, "and I will always remember it." For me, it had not seemed like a big deal but, for her, taking the time to recognize her and giving her a small tangible token of appreciation was a "magical memory." Oftentimes, just a simple "thank you," "great job," or "I'm proud of you" goes a long way.

 Action Points

> ▸ Think about how often you "blow your own horn" and how often you give others the credit.

- ▶ When things go right, do you take the credit or give credit to the team?
- ▶ Conversely, when things go wrong, whom do you blame?
- ▶ How often do you take the time to recognize the people who work for you, verbally and with small gifts?

 Payoff

Stronger teams, greater loyalty, a willingness to take risks, higher performance.

35. Bad Mood

Men decide far more problems by hate, love, lust,
rage, sorrow, joy, hope, fear, illusion, or some other
inward emotion, than by reality, authority, any
legal standard, judicial precedent or statute.
— CICERO

It is a youthful failing to be unable to control one's impulses.
— SENECA

A hot-tempered person stirs up conflict, but
the one who is patient calms a quarrel.
— BIBLE, PROVERBS 15:18

"What kind of mood is the boss in?" is a common question asked by workers in an organization. The answer often determines the kind of day that employees will experience. If the boss is in a good mood, everyone else usually is as well. But, if the boss is in a bad mood, watch out, as the team will follow suit.

The psychological term for this phenomenon is "emotional contagion." As humans, we tend to take on the emotions of people around us. The leader of the group has a disproportionate influence, as employees look to the leader for clues as to how they should behave.

The leader thus sets the emotional tone for her organization. If the leader is positive, affirming and enthusiastic, those around her will share these beneficial emotions. Although all organizations will profit from this, companies that depend on great customer service will particularly benefit, as employees reflect these emotions to customers.

As a leader, you need to learn to discipline your emotions. There were many times that I came to work tired or stressed, or became that way through the day. However, I refused to burden my team with my anger or anxiety. Having worked for hot-tempered bosses, I know the destructive, demoralizing influence of an emotionally uncontrolled leader.

Shortly after 9/11, one of my direct reports asked me how I was able to be so calm in Epcot's command center during the crisis. She commented that it was my second day on the job at Epcot, and that if she had been thrust into a situation like that, she didn't know if she would have reacted that well. I told her that I had experienced hundreds of emergency drills as a nuclear submarine officer, and that being in a command center during a crisis was almost second nature.

In a similar way, disciplining your emotions comes from daily awareness and practice. You should notice how your emotions impact others. Try going through the day in a very positive mood, and watch how well your team responds. At Disney, Cast Members are reminded that once you go "on-stage" (into areas that have Guests), you need to smile and be positive. There are even mirrors at backstage entrances with the phrase, "Are you wearing your smile?" As leaders, we are always "on-stage" and need to reflect that in our emotions.

Many companies have learned the high value of emotionally-disciplined leaders. Position descriptions for jobs often specify attributes such as "energetic," "positive" or "enthusiastic." Leaders with these attributes tend to draw out the best in their people and can face challenging situations boldly.

Surpassing leaders who discipline their emotions, refrain from bursts of anger and maintain a positive outlook are rewarded with highly productive, conquering teams that excel beyond measure.

 ## Action Points

- ▸ Remember that your emotions have a disproportionate impact on your people—as the leader, you establish the mood of the team.
- ▸ Be positive, affirming and enthusiastic, especially if you lead customer-facing areas.
- ▸ Discipline your emotions, and be particularly careful about displaying anger.

 ## Payoff

A positive, encouraging work environment, high morale for your team, outstanding interactions with customers.

36. The Yes Man

Those who agree with us may not be right,
but we admire their astuteness.
— CULLEN HIGHTOWER

Trust men and they will be true to you; treat them
greatly, and they will show themselves great.
— RALPH WALDO EMERSON

Captain John Butterworth was Chairman of the Political Science Department at the Naval Academy. He was a phenomenal, high energy leader who received twenty-one air medals plus the Distinguished Flying Cross, and was rumored to have a "secret life." Fluent in Farsi and having served as Naval Attache in Iran, he was noticeably absent during the 1980 Iranian hostage rescue attempt. When he returned, his white hair was dyed jet black. Many years later, it was confirmed that he was a member of the Delta Force for the rescue attempt.

I remember going to Captain Butterfield with a proposal when I attended the Academy. He responded, "Yes, absolutely do it!" and then said, "I always try to figure out how to say 'Yes!'"

Later in life, I realized that this was a secret of Captain Butterfield's success. Far too many leaders default to an answer of "No." They focus on all the potential downsides rather than the potential positives. New ideas take effort, money and time, all of which are often in short supply. The easiest answer is "No."

Reward systems typically favor a negative response. If a project is never approved, who will know if it would have been successful? But, if it is approved and fails, everyone will point fingers at the approving leader. Because of this, some leaders believe every "Yes" answer is high risk, and thus offer them very sparingly.

Surpassing leaders, on the other hand, perceive high value in every "Yes," and potential failure in every "No." Affirmative answers encourage new ideas and generate energy that often provides the time, money and resources to do the project. The best people gravitate toward leaders who try to find a way to say "Yes," and those people are the ones most likely to ensure a project is successful. With each success, more ideas flow, along with more great people and resources, and a greater probability of more successes.

I'm so glad for the many "yes" answers I have given in my career. One example is Epcot's Party for the Senses. Epcot hosts the International Food and Wine Festival for forty-five days in the fall. It is the world's largest and longest food and wine festival, amazingly held in a Disney theme park. Post 9/11, there were serious questions about whether the Festival would continue, and significant pressure to reduce the number of events during the Festival.

My team came to me with the idea of having a party during each Saturday night of the Festival. The party would have food stations with celebrity and Disney chefs, and wine stations featuring wineries that came to the Festival. The party would have a separate admission price on top of the cost for admission to Epcot. It was a great idea, but also risky, since we had no idea how many people would be willing to pay. The easy and safe answer would be to just say "No." But, remembering Captain Butterfield, I told the team to "Go for it!" and fought for the resources to make it happen. This unleashed amazing energy and creativity, and the Party for the Senses ultimately ended up with over twenty food stations, fifty wines, Cirque du Soleil entertainment and a reputation as the finest food and wine event in the world.

As you consider your leadership, do you tend to say "Yes" to new ideas, and challenge yourself and your team to make them happen? Take an affirmative approach and watch your leadership soar.

 ## Action Points

- Figure out how to say "Yes" to new ideas and proposals.
- Ensure your reward systems affirm taking risks, and don't just punish failures.
- Recognize that "Yes" answers can lead to the resources necessary to accomplish a project.

 ## Payoff

An exciting, fun, profitable workplace and life.

37.   1,000 Emails

The speed of the boss is the speed of the team.
— LEE IACOCCA

But you, Timothy, man of God: . . .
Run hard and fast in the faith.
— BIBLE, 1 TIMOTHY 6:11

It bugs me when I call or email someone and don't get a response. My mind considers the possibilities: Is their voice-mail or email not working? Is the person on vacation? Have I offended them and they are refusing to reply because of the offense? Then, a few days later, I'm forced into new decisions: Do I contact them again? If I called last time, should I use email this time? Should I check with someone else to find out if they are on vacation?

All of this would be unnecessary if people responded within twenty-four hours to their messages. I have set this as a personal goal, and find that it benefits me and the people who are contacting me in numerous ways:

▸ It strengthens my personal and business reputation. People know if they send me an email, I will respond, and respond quickly.
▸ It requires me to manage my schedule effectively, building in adequate time to reply expediently.
▸ It forces me to delegate in order to effectively manage the number of messages I receive.
▸ It prevents issues from escalating, as they are resolved swiftly.

- It reduces stress, as I don't have emails and calls building up over time.
- It is efficient, as I handle the issue immediately rather than putting it off and having to familiarize myself with it again later.
- It keeps me on top of rapidly changing situations rather than being several days behind others.

When I discuss twenty-four hour response, the usual retort is, "Sounds like a great idea, but there is no way I could ever do that with all the emails I get. I must get 1,000 emails a day!" I reply, "If you are getting 1,000 emails a day, you are either a significant micro-manager or on every spammers' address list."

If the quantity of emails you receive is overwhelming, you need to reduce it. Similar to the discussion in the Delegation section, you should critically review every email that you receive and decide:

- Do I absolutely have to handle this, or can I delegate it to someone else?
- Do I need this information on an on-going basis?
- Am I being "over-informed" by a person on my team, with many emails telling me everything they are doing in unnecessary detail?
- Is this junk email that I can stop by unsubscribing to it?

With a goal of responding in twenty-four hours, you can easily monitor your success and ruthlessly reduce your email to meet the target. You may find your emails significantly reduced, as people don't have to send you multiple follow-up messages since you are now responding quickly!

Action Points

- Commit to reply to your emails and messages within twenty-four hours.
- Put in place a process to ensure you meet your commitment.
- Reduce the number of emails that you get by critically reviewing each one.

 ## Payoff

Less stress, a strong professional reputation, greater productivity.

38. The Best Question Ever

A wise man's question contains half the answer.
— SOLOMON IBN GABIROL

*The important thing is not to stop questioning. Curiosity
has its own reason for existing. One cannot help but
be in awe when he contemplates the mysteries of
eternity, of life, of the marvelous structure of reality. It
is enough if one tries merely to comprehend a little of
this mystery every day. Never lose a holy curiosity.*
— ALBERT EINSTEIN

You do not have because you do not ask.
— BIBLE, JAMES 4:2

We have all had the experience. After a meal, the restaurant
manager walks up to our table and asks, "How was your dinner?"
The response is almost always the same: "Fine. Just fine"—even
if it was not. Most people don't want to cause conflict or get
into a lengthy critique. The manager walks away thinking there
are no problems, and the guest never returns.

The manager asked the wrong question. What she should
have asked is the best question ever: "What is the one thing
we could have done better?" If the guest responds, "Nothing.
There was not one thing you could have done better," then you
know you have a completely satisfied customer who will likely
return and will probably recommend your restaurant. Often,
though, a guest will mention something to improve: "The valet
was not there when I dropped off the car." "The soup was too

salty." "The service is slow." These comments are very useful and highly actionable.

Notice the careful wording: "What is the *one* thing *we could have done* better?" You ask for "one thing" not "anything." This requires the guest to prioritize the most important change they would like, and also informs that guest that they don't have to come up with a laundry list of issues. "We could have done" focuses the guest on an actionable item rather than an unattainable wish.

The same question can be used on a personal level to improve your leadership. You should constantly ask your employees, peers and superiors the question, "What is the one thing that I can do better?" You will get great ideas, and by acting on them, you can dramatically improve your performance and your team's execution.

Surpassing leaders constantly seek improvement for themselves and their teams. By asking the best question ever, these leaders learn about their opportunities and continuously advance and excel.

 ## Action Points

- ▸ Ask the best question ever, "What is the one thing that I/we can do better?"
- ▸ Teach your people to ask the question.
- ▸ Record and follow up on the response.

 ## Payoff

Strong, actionable feedback and significantly improved performance.

39. Who Cares?

I came to realize that life lived to help others is the
only one that matters and that it is my duty . . .
This is my highest and best use as a human.
— BEN STEIN

Help thy brother's boat across, and lo!
Thine own has reached the shore.
— HINDU PROVERB

For even the Son of Man did not come
to be served, but to serve . . .
— BIBLE, MARK 10:45

Many leadership books have addressed the topic of "servant leadership." In contrast to a top-down hierarchy where the purpose of the organization is to take care of the leader, servant leadership espouses the concept that the leader's role is to take care of the front line employees, so those employees can take care of customers.

The highest performance organizations in the world have this philosophy. In the United States Marine Corps, for example, officers eat after everyone else is fed. If there is not enough food, the officers don't eat. This sends a clear message that the officers' role is to take care of their subordinates first, rather than looking out for themselves.

Oftentimes, leaders attempt to use superior knowledge as the basis for their authority. As a Harvard Business school graduate, I was responsible for Harvard MBA recruiting for the Disney parks organization. We would typically hire about five top-tier MBAs per year. Many of them would leave within two years. As I did exit interviews and talked to the people who worked with and for these MBAs, a common theme was that "he was really smart, but he had trouble getting people to follow him." The MBA was usually task-oriented and emphasized her superior degree when challenged. Employees were driven hard, so the MBA could brag about the team output. The MBA jumped right into the work, spending little time developing relationships, common ground or loyalty. The result was frustration, disloyalty, resentment and ultimate failure.[13]

All of this could have been avoided if the book-smart MBA knew the common-sense expression: "People don't care how much you know, until they know how much you care." Leading others requires trust. If your people don't trust you, they won't follow you and, by definition, you will not be a leader. The best way to develop trust is by demonstrating to your followers that you care about them and have their best interest in mind. This doesn't mean that you are "soft" and allow poor performance. You can and should challenge and correct your people, but always with respect and appreciation.

The best way to show you care, respect and appreciate a person is to ask for their suggestions and then follow up on them. In employee roundtables, I would frequently hear, "My manager doesn't care about me." When I would probe for more details, the employee would say, "I told him about a problem and he never did anything about it." Most likely, the manager had forgotten to follow up, or had found out that he couldn't do

---

[13] I am pleased to say that Harvard Business School has recognized the issue and is focusing on developing humility in their students under the exceptional leadership of Dean Nitin Nohria, a man of humility and strong character.

anything and never responded back to the employee. Regardless, that manager betrayed trust and showed that he didn't care about the employee's problem.

Surpassing managers, on the other hand, constantly ask their people for suggestions and offer to help, then follow up. After seeing the difference between indifferent and helpful leaders, I decided to start answering my phone with a question: "Brad Rex, how can I help you?" This simple question immediately changes the dynamic of the call, and lets the caller know that my main goal is to assist him or her. Most people appreciate this attitude, which is much different than the more frequent response of indifference or even hostility.

 ## Action Points

- ▸ Would the people who work for you describe you as a "servant" leader?
- ▸ Do you demonstrate to your followers that you care about them and have their best interest in mind?
- ▸ Do you ask for suggestions?
- ▸ When suggestions are given, do you follow up on them?
- ▸ Do you ask people how you can help them?

 ## Payoff

Attracting the best people to work for you, a sense of satisfaction in helping others, high team morale and performance.

40. A Cup of Hot Chocolate

*The important thing is this: to be able at any moment
to sacrifice what we are for what we could become.*
— CHARLES DU BOS

*Decide what you want, decide what you are willing to
exchange for it. Establish your priorities and go to work.*
— H. L. HUNT

*In this life we get only those things for which we hunt, for
which we strive, and for which we are willing to sacrifice.*
— GEORGE MATTHEW ADAMS

I had just spoken at a Disney Leadership Conference when a young manager walked up to me. He introduced himself and said, "I don't expect that you remember me, but I worked at Epcot. I am a manager today because you gave me a cup of hot chocolate." My puzzled look encouraged him to continue with his story. "It was Christmas Eve and I had completed my night shift as the park closed. You were in the Cast hallway handing out cookies and cups of hot chocolate to the Cast Members as they were leaving. I knew you had young children, and that you had given up Christmas Eve with your kids to serve your Cast Members that night. I decided then that if that is what Disney leaders do, I wanted to be a Disney leader."

When many people look at leaders, they see the rewards of leadership—status, power, money, and privileges. Those rewards often motivate people to pursue leadership roles and "climb the corporate ladder." However, many don't recognize the sacrifices required in leadership. As I talk with aspiring leaders, I challenge them to ask the hard question: "Are you willing to make the sacrifices required to be a great leader?"

These sacrifices are immense. If you want to be a successful leader, you better be prepared to sacrifice. Oftentimes, your day will start when others are going home. You will be on call for customers, bosses, and your subordinates. Weekends become reserved for completing the work that was not finished during the week. You may need to move across the country or around the world. You will miss your children's games and other events. You will endure extreme stress, frustrating days and sleepless nights. As much as you might try to manage "work/life balance," you will face prolonged periods of imbalance when work is all consuming.

If you want to keep moving up, the choices become more and more difficult, as the increasing needs of your organization conflict with the increasing needs of your family. Oftentimes, these conflicting needs cause leaders to make poor choices that impact their companies and their families unnecessarily.

There are steps you can take as a leader to confront the issue of sacrifice. You need to recognize and commit to the sacrifice involved to attain great leadership, similar to the sacrifice required to become a great athlete. Professional athletes and Olympic champions know that the work is intense and long, while glory is fleeting. They commit, usually early in life, to excel in their sport, knowing that many other areas of life will have a lower priority. They also recognize that, despite their best efforts, they may not make the team, or could get injured before rising to prominence. Their families—parents, spouses, children—understand and accept the requirements and also commit to support them in their efforts.

Leaders in other areas need to make these same commitments and have the same understandings with their families. There should also be open discussions about limits. For the first thirteen years of my career, my wife and I were willing to move almost anywhere and at any time. We ended up moving eleven times in those thirteen years. Shortly after I started to work for Disney in Orlando, I was asked if I would move to California, for our twelfth move in fourteen years. With a three-year-old son and twin one-year-old daughters, my wife (justifiably) said no, and I agreed. During my twelve years at Disney, I was asked to move to France, California (several times), Tokyo and Hong Kong. The timing was not right from either a family standpoint (especially when my children were in high school) or due to community activities that I was leading. As I look back, it is clear that my career would have benefited from some of these moves. However, my family would have been impacted negatively. Leaders who don't set limits often make decisions they later regret, especially with regard to their spouses and families.

Leadership is a noble calling, with high rewards, but also high demands. If you aspire to lead, be prepared to sacrifice.

 Action Points

> ► Recognize that leadership requires sacrifice, and the higher you wish to lead, the more you will have to sacrifice.
> ► Ensure you are committed to make leadership a priority, and that your family will support you.

▶ Be willing to set limits, especially as they relate to your family.

 ## Payoff

A full commitment to excel as a leader, open communication, and no regrets later in life.

41.   Santa Claus and The Elf

I think we're having fun. I think our customers really like
our products. And we're always trying to do better.
— STEVE JOBS

If you never did, you should. These
things are fun and fun is good.
— DR. SEUSS

When you have confidence, you can have a lot of fun.
And when you have fun, you can do amazing things.
— JOE NAMATH

The average person living to age seventy has 613,000
hours of life. This is too long a period not to have fun.
— AUTHOR UNKNOWN

As part of the preparation for the Naval Nuclear Power Program Engineer's Exam, candidates meet with different submarine commanding officers to be quizzed and learn about the most unique situation the CO had ever faced. After a few questions and stories, one of the captains told me about his leadership style. He said, "If you aren't having fun, you aren't doing it right!" I was somewhat taken aback by his comment in the middle of a very serious discussion. But, as I thought about it, I realized that his boat was the top performer in our squadron, and his crew had high morale.

I worked for an outstanding executive at British Petroleum named Paul Vaight. Paul was a brilliant man who had a tremendous sense of humor. He was always laughing, and help-ing others to laugh. At the time, he had one of the worst jobs at BP, as the financial controller for a $50 billion company that was in the midst of massive restructuring. He frequently had to share bad news with BP's Chairman and CEO. As a team, we worked very long hours supporting Paul. Yet, we had fun and maintained strong esprit de corps thanks to Paul's humor.

In my leadership roles, I have always tried to make work fun. We spend far too many of our waking hours at work for it to be so serious. Some leaders believe that work should always be serious, and any "fun" should take place after hours. The facts prove otherwise, with happier employees boosting returns. Based on a study by Alex Edmans of the Wharton School, companies listed in *Fortune*'s "100 Best Companies to Work For in America" had 3.5 percent higher equity returns per year than those of their peers over a twenty-five year period.[14] One of the key determinants of employee satisfaction is having fun at work—fun does equate to financial success.

There are many ways to inject fun into work, but I have found one of the best is to have the leader dress up in an unusual costume. I have been Elvis, an elf, Santa Claus, a surfer dude, a Roman statesman (in a toga, of course), a pirate, and countless other characters.

When I led one of the major finance teams at Disney, I was responsible for the monthly Cast Member recognition program. Turnout had been sparse, and interest in the program was dwindling. The recognition team asked me if I would be willing to dress in a costume if they came up with a theme for

---

[14] Edmans, Alex, Does the Stock Market Fully Value Intangibles? Employee Satisfaction and Equity Prices (January 20, 2010). *Journal of Financial Economics* (JFE), Forthcoming.

each month. I agreed and we soon had a packed crowd, eager to find out if Brad was really going to deliver as promised, such as dressing up as a ladybug for the Spring Fling. (I was a pretty good looking ladybug, if I do say so myself!) Each time was immense fun for the team and created a lasting memory. Many years later, I have had employees reminisce about these events; "I remember when you dressed up like Elvis for the awards ceremony."

While some leaders might refuse this approach and say it is "undignified," I have found people have greater respect for a leader who has the confidence to serve his or her team by putting on an outlandish costume. Surpassing leaders of the best-performing companies make having fun a high priority, and create a fun working environment.

 ## Action Points

- ▸ Make your work environment fun.
- ▸ The more intense the pressure, the more important it is to inject fun.
- ▸ Dress up in a costume, especially for recognition programs and holiday videos.

 ## Payoff

Improved morale, more satisfied employees, a reputation as a confident, respected leader.

42. Follow the Leader

*The true test of your leadership is whether what
you start continues on after you are gone.*
—Dr. Rocco Paone,
United States Naval Academy Professor

In my last year at the Naval Academy, Dr. Paone shared this thought with me, and encouraged me to ponder how I could achieve this in my life. I found the best way to fulfill this challenge is to train your successor. This is critical for the organization and your career, as "there is no success without a successor."

I would modify this phrase to "there is often no promotion without a successor." Some people have the mistaken notion that, if no one can take their place, they will have job security and advancement. However, I have participated in many talent talks/promotion discussions and found that leaders are often rejected for new roles because there is no one to take their place. If there are two candidates for promotion, the candidate who has prepared a successor to easily take his place is greatly preferred over a candidate whose area would be placed in turmoil if he left.

In my organizations, I have required my leaders to identify at least one and preferably two people who can take their place. This ensured solid bench strength and ongoing mentorship. We could readily absorb turnover created by promotions. My areas were known as a great "hunting ground" for talent. In a virtuous cycle, we attracted the best people who were seeking advancement, trained them, required them to train their successor, and then promoted them. As they were promoted and their successor took their place, other top talent came in behind and filled that slot. We consistently had the best performers and most productive teams.

As a leader, you will be judged by the continuing success of your operation after you leave. Will you leave your team in good hands?

From both a personal and organizational standpoint, selecting and training successors leads to greater opportunities, compensation and returns.

 ## Action Points

> ▸ Can you name at least one, and preferably two, people who you are training to be your successor?
> ▸ If you lead others, can your people do the same?
> ▸ Is your team known as a great hunting ground for talent?
> ▸ Will your team thrive or collapse when you leave?

 ## Payoff

More advancement opportunities, greater success, a network of incredible leaders and friends.

43. Harsh Critics

Never underestimate the power of the irate customer.
— JOEL E. ROSS

*Blessed are the peacemakers, for they
will be called children of God.*
— BIBLE, MATTHEW 5:9

All leaders will be called upon to deal with irate people at some point. By nature, leaders foster change, which is resisted by some who become angry when they are forced to change. Sometimes an organization screws up, and the leader must face irate customers. I have found a good approach to dealing with an angry person, especially a customer, is the LAST Chance model.

The LAST Chance model has four components: Listen, Apologize, Solve and Thank. You first Listen to the irate person and use the active listening technique discussed in Chapter 4. If someone is particularly angry, let them vent without interruption until they finally stop. Then paraphrase back to them the issue and how it made them feel.

Next, you apologize. This is easy if you or your organization made a mistake, and the person has a cause to be angry. It is harder to apologize if the person caused the problem or the situation is beyond your control (e.g., an event was rained out). However, you can always apologize for the way the person is feeling ("I apologize that you are upset that the event was rained out.")

Then, you attempt to solve the issue. You should ask the person for their solution: "How do you think we should resolve this issue?" or "What do you want me to do about the situation?"

Many leaders are very afraid to ask this question, as they expect outlandish demands ("You should pay for my entire vacation and give me a free return trip."). From my experience, most people are very reasonable, and often don't ask for any type of compensation ("I'm not looking for anything, I just wanted to make sure someone knew about the issue."). Their solution may surprise you: "I'd just like you to make reservations for us for tomorrow night." On the rare occasion when someone demands an excessive solution, you can challenge it and say, "We need to find a reasonable solution that works for both of us. I am willing to . . ."

The last, and most important step is to thank the person for bringing the issue to your attention. For ten dissatisfied customers, only one or two will typically complain. The other eight or nine will likely just never return and will tell their friends about the poor experience. With the people who complain, you should be able to recover their experience.

Surpassing leaders use the LAST Chance technique to handle difficult situations. Listen, Apologize, Solve, and Thank can turn a harsh critic into a strong advocate.

 Action Points

- ► Are you ready to deal with an angry person?
- ► Apply the LAST chance model to your next difficult encounter—Listen, Apologize, Solve, Thank.
- ► Make sure your people are prepared by teaching and role playing the LAST chance model.

 Payoff

Making strident critics into raving fans!

165

44. Behind Closed Doors

*The day soldiers stop bringing you their problems is the
day you have stopped leading them. They have either
lost confidence that you can help them or concluded that
you do not care. Either case is a failure of leadership.*
— COLIN POWELL

*This is the confidence we have in approaching God: that
if we ask anything according to his will, he hears us.*
— BIBLE, 1 JOHN 5:14

My assistant came into my office and closed the door. I knew
that was not a good sign. "You have a problem," she started.
"I have many problems!" I replied, but noticed that she didn't
smile at my weak humor. "People are interrupting you all the
time while you are trying to work. Any Cast Member who walks
by your office thinks they can just drop in and talk to you."
I listened as she continued, "From now on, I'm going to tell
people they need an appointment to see you. I'll only schedule
Cast Members during certain times of the day so you can get
your work done without anyone interrupting you."

From a time management standpoint, her plan made sense.
You are more productive when you can focus on the task at hand
without interruption. However, from a leadership standpoint,
being approachable and accessible is far more valuable than
uninterrupted paperwork time. I told her, "Thank you for being
concerned about me and coming up with a solution. However,
these interruptions *are* my work—not the paperwork. Because
Cast Members can freely come to me, I have a much better

166

sense of what is happening in the park. They bring me small problems before they become big problems. I get suggestions, compliments, and complaints directly, without any filtering. If you tell people they need appointments, many won't come back. I'll lose my 'listening posts' and very valuable information. And, I'll gain a reputation for being unapproachable."

While I could have eaten at my desk or with other executives in a Disney restaurant, I chose to eat in the Cast Member cafeteria. This gave me a great opportunity to informally chat with the Cast. I got to know many Cast Members, and they became comfortable being around me. They would tell me about an issue and I would update them the next time I saw them at lunch. I would also often buy the lunch of the person in line ahead of me, as a way to "surprise and delight" our Cast, as we expected them to surprise and delight our Guests. One day, I bought lunch for an International Program Cast Member. It was apparent she had no idea who I was or why in the world I would be buying her lunch. I think she thought it was a unique American custom to buy a stranger's meal. She later found out who I was and sent me a note of thanks. She said it was her first day at Epcot and she left that lunch thinking about the wonderful place where she would be working.

Surpassing leaders need to spend the time and effort to reach *all* their people. Epcot had Guests or Cast Members in the park twenty-four hours a day, 365 days a year. Many Custodial and Engineering Cast Members worked the third shift, in the middle of the night. I would show up unannounced to get to know them and see how they were doing. The usual response was, "What are you doing here?" with a quizzical look. It made for a long day afterward, but was invaluable in building trust and open communication.

Are you approachable as a leader? Do you purposely spend time out with your people, or do you stay behind closed doors? Do your employees come to you with problems, or are you assuming everything is great because you never hear any complaints? Leaders who exceed beyond all expectations are highly approachable, trusted and connected to their organizations.

 ## Action Points

- How frequently are you contacted with issues? If you aren't receiving much feedback, don't assume you have no problem.
- Is it easy for people to meet with you? If not, remove the barriers.
- Do you frequently eat lunch at your desk or do you use lunchtime as the opportunity to meet with others in your organization?
- If your organization has employees who come in earlier or later, how often do you see them?

 ## Payoff

An "early warning system" for problems, a better idea of what is truly happening at your company, great relationships with your employees.

45. Be Nice to Strangers

Be hospitable.
— HILTON HOTEL MOTTO

Rather, he must be hospitable,
one who loves what is good,
who is self-controlled, upright,
holy and disciplined.
— BIBLE, TITUS 1:8

Conrad Hilton, the founder of the Hilton hotel chain, was an avid reader of the Bible. We can only surmise that he decided to use this source in determining the motto for his hotel chain. In describing the qualifications of a leader when writing to Titus, Paul lists five negatives—qualities that a leader should not have, such as a quick temper or someone who seeks dishonest gain. He then gives six positives, and the first is "be hospitable," which ranks above being holy and disciplined. Why is hospitality so important for a great leader?

We get the word for hospitality from the Greek term, philo-xenos, which is a combination of philos, or friend, and xenos, or stranger. Someone who is hospitable is a "friend of strangers." It describes one who is generous, welcoming and friendly to visitors, guests and strangers, giving practical help to anyone in need.

Leaders are expected to treat their people well. But, how well do they treat strangers? Whether from a childhood experience of being told not to talk to strangers, aloofness due to position, busyness, introversion or complacency, many leaders are not hospitable, and can even be considered antagonistic.

The behavior of a leader toward strangers is often a good indicator of character. Is he dismissive of others? Does she display distrust of outsiders? Or, is she positive and cordial, attentive to needs and open to new ideas?

The surpassing leader highly values strangers. He knows there is no such thing as a stranger—only a potential new customer, partner or employee. She also knows that strangers bring knowledge and experience that can be very helpful. Strangers also bring entire new networks, expanding the leader's influence.

King Solomon was known as the wisest man on earth during his lifetime. You would think that he would have no use for strangers. Yet, he was very welcoming of guests, especially those from distant lands. His wisdom told him it was wise to be hospitable.

As you are hospitable, your people will follow your lead and they will learn and grow, strengthening your organization.

Do you have a reputation for being hospitable? If you desire to lead beyond measure, go out of your way to be friendly to strangers.

 ## Action Points

- Are you welcoming and friendly to strangers?
- Do you reach out to others, or do you expect them to reach out to you?
- Is your organization known for hospitality?

 ## Payoff

New partners, friends, customers and employees, greater wisdom, more far reaching networks.

CHAPTER 7

Success Beyond Measure

---

*The truth is that all of us attain the greatest success
and happiness possible in this life whenever we use
our native capacities to their greatest extent.*
— DR. SMILEY BLANTON

*He has achieved success who has lived well,
laughed often and loved much.*
— BESSIE A. STANLEY

*Success is liking yourself, liking what you
do, and liking how you do it.*
— MAYA ANGELOU

THROUGH SURPASSING LIVING, you have become healthy
and wealthy; gained a reputation for honor and honesty;
developed new, strong relationships; filled your mind with knowledge; and, reached new levels of leadership. Most people would
be ecstatic with these results. Yet, there are further opportunities
to practice surpassing principles and achieve lasting success.

46.   Ten Million Hits

*If a man is called to be a street sweeper, he should sweep
streets even as Michelangelo painted, or Beethoven composed
music, or Shakespeare wrote poetry. He should sweep streets
so well that all the hosts of heaven and earth will pause to
say, here lived a great street sweeper who did his job well."*
— MARTIN LUTHER KING, JR.

*Do you see someone skilled in their work?
They will serve before kings.*
— BIBLE, PROVERBS 22:29A

I do my work with wisdom, knowledge, and skill.
— BIBLE, ECCLESIASTES 2:21

There is a direct relationship between excellence and income.
People who are excellent in a particular area will be in demand.
Since excellence is in short supply, as long as you are excellent
in a field that is useful to society, you will have work and be
rewarded. When I was a teenager thinking about my future,
my father told me, "I don't care what job you pursue, just be
the best one out there." His words had special credibility, as he
was a world-class ear surgeon who piloted innovative techniques
to restore hearing. While what you choose to do is important,
deciding to do it with excellence will ensure long-term satisfaction and compensation.

Excellence can be grasped, but not acquired. You can
become first in your class in high school, but then, the day after

graduation, you have to reset your goal to become first in college. In a profession, you may achieve excellence momentarily, but will have to learn new skills to continue to stay on top. Here are a few practical ideas to pursue excellence:

- Set your goal to be the best, and commit to spending the time and energy to get there. Most people set their goals too low and settle for mediocre results. With a goal to be number one, even if you don't make it, you'll be in the top group. When I went to the Naval Academy, I set a goal to be first in my class. I spent countless hours studying and striving to be the best. I didn't get to number one, but I did graduate fifth out of 935, which was more than satisfying.
- Be a lifelong learner. There are always new ideas to learn and try. Leaders, for example, should always be reading a leadership book. If you Google the term "leadership books," you'll get over ten million hits. There are plenty to choose from, and you have no excuse for not having something to read.
- Always search for a better way. Take best practices from others and improve on them. Challenge yourself and your team to be faster, better, smarter. Look at problems as opportunities.
- Stay humble. Although it sounds like a contradiction in terms, humble experts realize that they don't know everything, and must be willing to learn from others.
- Experiment constantly. Doctors "practice" medicine, meaning they are always trying new procedures and medicines to achieve better outcomes. Similarly, you should try new ideas and ways of doing things, both personally and professionally.
- Foster personal creativity. Excellent performers provide creative solutions to problems—new approaches that no one

has considered. This requires having different experiences—books, travel, relationships—outside your normal area of expertise, and applying those experiences to problem areas.

Excellence begets excellence. As you become known for excellence, other people of excellence will join you, as leaders, peers, friends and mentors challenging you to be better. You'll have an excellent life.

 ## Action Points

- ▶ Set your goals to be the best in your chosen area and do the work to get there.
- ▶ Read constantly—always have a book with you.
- ▶ Look for problems and solve them.
- ▶ Learn from others.
- ▶ Try new things.
- ▶ Have different experiences.

 ## Payoff

Personal excellence, professional success, wealth and a fascinating, exciting life!

47.   The Best Leadership Book

Keep this Book of the Law always on your lips; meditate on it day and night, so that you may be careful to do everything written in it. Then you will be prosperous and successful.
— BIBLE, JOSHUA 1:8

I am frequently asked, "What is the best leadership book?" My answer is always the Bible. I have read thousands of leadership books and articles, and can attest that every leadership principle espoused by the authors can be found in a story or proverb from the Bible. This is why I tell leaders to go directly to the source to find the most concise and comprehensive information to enhance their leadership.

The Bible is the best-selling book of all time. It is also the most widely quoted book. Biblical references and expressions are used by writers, politicians, public speakers, athletes, newscasters, bloggers, editorialists, historians and, of course, pastors. The most influential leaders of the last few centuries relied extensively on the Bible, including Martin Luther King, Gandhi, Abraham Lincoln and almost all US Presidents, generals, college presidents and CEOs. Whatever your spiritual beliefs, as an educated person and leader, you should read the Bible and the leadership stories that it reveals.

Reading the Bible can help strengthen character virtues. To strengthen integrity, you can read the story of Daniel and the benefits of a life lived with integrity. David and Esther evidence courage. Joseph shows determination and forgiveness. Abraham and Noah show obedience and persistent faith. Job demonstrates perseverance through adversity. The Bible also provides lists of favorable character traits to emulate, like generosity, peacemaking, self-control, moderation, forbearance, kindness, goodness and joy.

We also see warnings about behaviors that derail leaders. Although he was "a man after God's own heart," David ignored his family and fell prey to lust and adultery. Solomon's wisdom didn't protect him when he succumbed to wealth and women. Numerous characters allowed pride to destroy their judgment and their careers. Judas betrayed his leader, Jesus, for money and politics, while Peter betrayed Jesus under fear of arrest.

As a leader, you will be faced many times when things "don't make sense." Business efforts will fail despite the best planning and execution. People who work for you will die, sometimes in tragic ways. Close friends will betray you. Someone else will get promoted over you. Your work life may be thriving, while your personal life is in ruin. The Bible helps to put these situations into perspective, gives you words to comfort the grieving or lost, and provides hope in the midst of adversity.

Specifically, what will you say or do when you face a death—of an employee, an employee's spouse, parent or child, or a customer? I guarantee that you will be in this situation at some point in your leadership. Beyond "I'm sorry," do you have any words to help those who grieve? I have a condolence letter based on Biblical principals that I have sent to those in grief, and have received many comments that my words were helpful and comforting in a difficult time.

The Bible describes good and bad leaders. The story of Nehemiah details the entire process a leader goes through in starting and completing a major project, including dealing with opposition and what to do when the people you leave in charge lead inappropriately. Every leader can learn from Nehemiah the critical elements of project leadership. The story of Jesus shows how a leader who is born in the lowest circumstances can impact the world for over 2,000 years. Weak leaders include Saul, who attempted to kill his successor, David, to maintain the throne. Young King Rehoboam ignored the advice of his elders and instead listened to the youth he had grown up with, resulting in a rebellion against his rule. Pontius Pilate gave in to mob rule and ordered Jesus to be crucified, then "washed his hands" of the decision. Each story provides leaders with invaluable insight into the consequences of human behavior, especially their own.

I attempt to read the Bible daily and it is amazing to me how often my reading for the day helps me with a situation that is happening in my life or that arises during that day. If you have never read the Bible, it might appear a daunting task. Although most people have heard of the King James Version and may start with that, I suggest you get a contemporary version, such as the New International Version or the Message, which is much easier to read and understand. Some Bibles are arranged for daily reading of about fifteen to twenty minutes, with a passage from the Old Testament, a passage from the New Testament, a Psalm and a Proverb. These provide interesting variety and allow you to read through the entire Bible in a year. I would challenge you to give this a try and find out if your reading supports you in your daily interactions.

Surpassing leaders pursue wisdom, and the best source is the wisest book ever written—the Bible.

Action Points

- ▸ Read the Bible on a regular basis, preferably a few times a week or even daily.
- ▸ Study the characters and look for parallels to people you may meet in your work and personal life.
- ▸ Get strength from the stories of perseverance and courage.
- ▸ Enhance your character by studying the examples of good and bad decisions.

Payoff

Wisdom, strength, courage, perspective, peace.

48. Shhhh

*In the attitude of silence the soul finds the path in
a clearer light, and what is elusive and deceptive
resolves itself into crystal clearness. Our life is
a long and arduous quest after Truth.*
— MAHATMA GANDHI

*I have discovered that all human evil comes from
this; man's being unable to sit still in a room.*
— BLAISE PASCAL

*When you don't know what to do, get still. Get
very still until you do know what to do.*
— OPRAH WINFREY

Be still and know that I am God.
— BIBLE, PSALM 46:10

Phone calls. Emails. Text messages. Commercials. Billboards.
Pop-ups. Multi-tasking. 24/7. Single parents. Sandwich generation. Instant messaging. On demand. In today's world, we are
constantly bombarded by messages, activity and demands.

Contrast this with our forebears from a generation ago, who
"lacked" our modern conveniences of cellphones, computers,
microwaves and cable television. Most stores were open nine to
five and everything was closed on Sundays, by law. There were
only three TV channels, businesses communicated by letters,
memos and faxes, and phones were wired to the wall. People
took vacations (often for several weeks) and did not work.

A huge benefit of this lifestyle was the freedom of thought time, without distraction. Watching a sunset, taking a walk after dinner, enjoying a lazy Sunday afternoon in the hammock, or completely forgetting about work on vacation was an expectation, rather than an exception.

Interestingly, the United States enjoyed its highest productivity from 1870–1950, with the greatest growth from 1930–1950. Current growth pales in comparison. The statistic of "multifactor productivity," which measures the benefit of new ideas, has been essentially flat since the 1970s, compared to two to three percent per year during the 1950s and 1960s. While there are many potential causes, could the lack of quiet, reflective time reduce our capacity for innovation?

Despite the pressures of our society, you can set boundaries that allow you to put thinking time back into your schedule:

▸ Set aside time each day on your calendar for reflection. Many people do this in the morning prior to getting ready for work or school. Some read the Bible or a morning devotional. Others walk and think. Scientific studies have shown significant benefits from combining physical activity, changing natural scenery and pondering a problem.[15]

▸ Prior to dinner, have everyone put his or her mobile device in a basket (preferably soundproof) and leave it there for the duration. For once, you can have an uninterrupted conversation.

▸ Put your mobile device in another room when you get home from work and don't look at it the rest of the night.

---

[15] "Exercise alone provides psychological and physical benefits. However, if you also adopt a strategy that engages your mind while you exercise, you can get a whole host of psychological benefits fairly quickly." James Rippe, MD

- Turn off the radio in the car during your commute.
- Establish a TV-free night on at least one day during the week.
- Set an out-of-office alert and turn off your email on vacation. One of the best vacations we took as a family was an overseas cruise. I told everyone in the family that I would not pay international roaming charges and all phones had to stay off during the entire trip. We focused on each other and put aside the hectic expectation of immediately responding to others.
- Set one day of your week, such as Saturday or Sunday, as a "Sabbath," when you rest, relax and don't do any work. Use the time to reflect and reconnect with friends and family.

As you think back on the times when you were most productive and had your best ideas, you'll likely find it was when you were not at work. Be sure to create "downtimes" to maximize your creativity and productivity.

 ## Action Points

- Set boundaries for yourself and your family.
- Determine your best time or environment for ideas, and replicate it.
- Recognize that a rhythm of work and rest results in greater productivity, and constant activity results in diminishing returns.

 ## Payoff

Better ideas, a more relaxed life, stronger family connections, more innovation.

49. Put Family First

If you ever start feeling like you have the goofiest, craziest, most dysfunctional family in the world, all you have to do is go to a state fair. Because five minutes at the fair, you'll be going, "You know, we're alright. We are dang near royalty."
— JEFF FOXWORTHY

Call it a clan, call it a network, call it a tribe, call it a family. Whatever you call it, whoever you are, you need one.
— JANE HOWARD

It is dismal coming home, when there is nobody to welcome one!
— ANN RADCLIFFE

Honor your father and your mother, so that you may live long in the land the LORD your God is giving you.
— BIBLE, EXODUS 20:12,
THE FIFTH COMMANDMENT

Children's children are a crown to the aged, and parents are the pride of their children.
— BIBLE, PROVERBS 17:6

When we moved to Florida and I had my first role with Disney, I worked long hours in an effort to get ahead. My career had always been a driving force. We had three children, a son and twin daughters, who were all under three years of age ("three under three"). We were active in our church. With all of our busyness, my wife and I were moving apart in our marriage. We weren't fighting—we just weren't engaging.

I went to hear the chairman of a major banking system in Florida speak at an Lifework Leadership event. He was everything I wanted to be—very successful financially, well regarded in the community, powerful and influential. I was hoping his talk would be about how to achieve a life like his. Instead, he talked about the failure of his marriage due to his neglect. He said he would give anything to go back and restore that relationship. His words echoed in my mind as I drove home: "If you fail with your family, you fail in life."

At that point, I recognized the importance of people and my interactions with them, and put more emphasis on my wife and family. Yet, I soon fell back to old habits and started to miss dinners and events with my children. Then, I read a *Wall Street Journal* article in which the author interviewed very successful CEOs. He asked them what they would do differently if they could do it all over again. One CEO said he had missed many family events because of work requirements. His quote greatly impacted me: "You will never remember the business emergency, but you will always remember the missed ball game and piano recital."

From that day on, I looked at my commitments to my family in the same way as if I had an important business meeting with my boss. It often meant that I had to work late into the night after the ball game or awards ceremony, but being true to commitments to my family was the right choice.

You have a job for years, but you have your family for life. With children, the most important times in their lives and when parents have the greatest influence are the pre-school years and their high school years. I have talked to many friends who had commuting or high-travel jobs during their children's high school years, and deeply regretted it. Although some youth rebel during that time and act like they aren't listening, they are actually being heavily influenced by what you say and, more particularly, how you act. They are facing critical decisions about daily temptations and longer-term college and career choices. Being present to help them navigate through these issues gives them a solid foundation for their future. If you have to give up a promotion to stay home more during those years, you'll likely find it a worthy trade-off.

The "sandwich generation" describes many baby boomers who are taking care of both children and aging parents. As baby boomers delayed having children and their parents are living much longer lives, more boomers are "sandwiched" than ever before. Busy jobs, participating in teenagers' full schedules, and supporting the needs of parents can create tremendous time stress. Financial stress can also ensue, as some parents outlive their savings (especially if they have significant chronic illnesses), and must depend on their children, who are spending heavily on their own families, particularly if they have college-age children. A key opportunity for baby boomers in this situation is to demonstrate love and honor for their parents. The children will see their example, and hopefully follow it when their parents are elderly.

It takes effort and sacrifice to keep a family together. Those who want to really excel and succeed in life take on this challenge and reap lifetime benefits.

Action Points

- ▸ Treat commitments to your family with the same priority as work and other commitments.
- ▸ Recognize the importance of being present for your children, especially in their teenage years.
- ▸ Honor your parents so your children can learn from your example.

Payoff

Strong family relationships, successful children, a worthy legacy.

50.   Thanks!

Gratitude is not only the greatest of virtues,
but the parent of all others.
— CICERO

I would maintain that thanks are the highest form of thought,
and that gratitude is happiness doubled by wonder.
— G.K. CHESTERTON

Give thanks to the LORD, for he is
good: his love endures forever.
— BIBLE, 1 CHRONICLES 16:34

Have you ever been with people who have very little, but seem very happy and satisfied? The lack of material things may make them appear to be unsuccessful by our culture's definition, yet most millionaires would envy their happiness. They have achieved surpassing success through gratitude.

Our culture teaches us to regret the things we don't have, rather than be thankful for the things we do. This is a marketing strategy to drive demand. "You'll be sorry if you don't buy these shoes." "You'll regret not getting the girl if you don't drink this beer." "You will miss out on life if you don't have this car." The constant barrage of remorseful messages creates fear and anxiety that drains the energy from life, since there will always be things we don't have.

A thankful person reverses this thinking. She looks at what she has, rather than what she lacks. She actually realizes that she has many things to be thankful for, and the more things she lists, the more that come to mind.

The unthankful person often makes comparisons. "He has more money or a bigger house." "She is prettier or thinner than I am." The unthankful person forgets that life is a package deal. The person who is rich may have destroyed his family. The woman who is thin may have an eating disorder or multiple food allergies. The person who is famous has no privacy. After reading that Bill Gates' children required bodyguards to go to school, my children told me, "We're glad you're a nobody, Dad." I'm not sure exactly how to take that, but I accepted it as a compliment. No one "has it all"—there are always negatives with positives. As you look at someone and say, "I wish I had their life," remember what you would have to give up, and the negatives that come with the positives. You will decide that your life is just fine, and be thankful for what you have.

With the adverse pressures of our culture, fostering an "attitude of gratitude" requires effort. Several practices can help. The first is a simple list of the things that you are thankful for. You can start with various headings, such as health, family, food, shelter, and then build on each topic (e.g., for health—life, the ability to walk, sight, taste, etc.; family—spouse, children, parents, siblings). You can build up a lengthy list quickly, and realize just how fortunate you are. Pull out the list every day and give thanks for a few things. If you get disappointed in an area, like losing a promotion or ending a relationship, look at the list and realize how good things are going in other areas of your life.

Robert A. Emmons, a professor at the University of California, Davis, and Michael E. McCullough at the University of Miami conducted research showing that listing five things for which you are grateful with a sentence for each once a week had a profound effect within two months. Versus a control group, the "gratitude group" were more optimistic and happy, spent more time exercising and had fewer physical problems. They also fell asleep faster, had a longer sleep and reported waking up feeling more refreshed. Instead of a sleeping pill, try a gratitude journal!

You can also create a personal marker chronology. This shows how the events that have happened to you or the decisions that you made have positively benefited your life. You should start with your birthplace and upbringing. You might have had an idyllic early life that gave you many benefits and a positive outlook. Or, your early years could have been a struggle that taught you resilience and street smarts. Your choice of college, military or a job after high school sent your life in a particular direction. The places you lived, down to the specific neighborhoods, determined your friends and activities. If you had children, you can see the timing and how that fit into the rest of your life.

A personal marker chronology provides perspective. When you broke up with your high school or college sweetheart that you thought was "the one," you were probably devastated. Your chronology, though, will show that the break-up resulted in meeting your future spouse and a much better life. Similarly, the lost job at one point resulted in a much better job or location later. When the next "bad" thing happens to you, you can look at your chronology and be thankful, realizing that what initially looks bad often leads to a future positive outcome.

Success without gratitude is a hollow victory, and often short-lived. With the next challenge or disappointment, the successful ingrate quickly folds, finding that the previous success provides little assurance or comfort. On the other hand, the thankful person enjoys their current success, while recognizing that the situation can change, and has the resilience to give thanks in all circumstances.

 Action Points

- ► Be thankful for what you have, not regretful for what you lack.
- ► Don't make comparisons or, if you do, remember the other person's life is a "package deal"—you have to take their bad with the good.
- ► Develop an attitude of gratitude.
- ► Make a list of the things you are thankful for and review it often.
- ► Gain perspective from a personal marker chronology.

 Payoff

A much happier life, positive outlook and resilience in challenging times.

51. Humble Success

Now the man Moses was a quietly humble man,
more so than anyone living on Earth.
— BIBLE, NUMBERS 12:3

Humble success sounds like an oxymoron. Usually, success results in pride, not humility. We often associate humility with lowliness and failure. The word humility is translated tapeinophrosune in Greek, meaning "to think or judge with lowliness." Yet, long-term surpassing success only comes from humility.

Jim Collins makes the business case for humility in describing the highest level of leader, the Level 5 leader in his book, *Good to Great: Level 5 leaders are ambitious first and foremost for the cause, the organization, the work—not themselves—and they have the fierce resolve to do whatever it takes to make good on that ambition. A Level 5 leader displays a paradoxical blend of* **personal humility** *and professional will.*

The prideful person often falls prey to one of the following "derailers":

1. **"My hard work got me here."** I struggled with this until the day I worked at a homeless shelter. I sat down to lunch with one of the men and heard his story. As he described growing up fatherless, with a drug addicted mother in a crime-infested neighborhood, I realized that I would have likely been homeless if I had the same experience. We don't choose the family we are born into and, as you look back, you will probably see some key times when you got a "break" that determined your future. Hard work is important, but

so is intelligence, ambition, appearance, upbringing and family—all things that are outside your control.

2. **Personal competitiveness.** I'm a very competitive person, which is a blessing and a curse. Competitiveness can motivate you to take risks and excel, but it can also drive you to make poor choices. Before the recession, the *Wall Street Journal* used to have a section highlighting job promotions. I always read it with interest, looking first for the person's name to see if I knew them, then the new position and company, and finally their age. I would compare their age to mine to see if I was "on-track." If the person was younger than me and at a higher level, my competitiveness would kick in, and it would be time to call the recruiters. C.S. Lewis, famous for his treatises on pride, wrote: *Pride gets no pleasure out of having something, only out of having more than the next man.* If you are never satisfied, you will do anything to get more, and your success will be short-lived.

3. **Flattery and infallibility.** When I took over at Epcot, all of a sudden my jokes became much funnier. This is a form of flattery. Many who succeed believe "success breeds success," and their decisions cannot fail. Successful people often start "smoking their own exhaust" and believe their flatterers, until a misjudgment derails them.

4. **"I am irreplaceable."** Successful leaders sometimes delude themselves into believing their organizations will fail if they leave. In their mind, this delusion means they must do anything possible to remain in their role, to "save the company." They fire potential successors, create organizational turmoil, and engage in bitter proxy fights. Often, they put the company at risk, and the only way to save it is to fire them.

5. **Temptation.** Successful people can believe that they are less prone to temptation or, if they succumb, their fame or money will protect them. Ancient wisdom is as pertinent today as 2,000 years ago: *If you think you are standing strong, be careful, for you, too, may fall into the same sin. But remember that the temptations that come into your life are no different from what others experience.*[16] A good example is former Governor and Attorney General for the State of New York, Elliot Spitzer. He had money, power and fame. He thought he was above temptation (or at least getting caught) and succumbed to the temptation of engaging prostitutes, derailing his success.

Humble success is possible in today's business world. The finest leader I ever had the pleasure to work for is Judson Green. Judson is an incredible "Renaissance Man" who was Chairman of Disney's Parks and Resorts division. He transformed the culture of the division, and led the company through five years of double-digit revenue and income growth, achieving six billion dollars in revenue. He then went on to become Chief Executive Officer of NAVTEQ, a preeminent mapping software company, taking the company public and then selling it to Nokia. Beyond his substantial business success, Judson is a concert-level jazz pianist and composer.

Judson epitomizes the Level 5 leader who cares about the people who work for him, and builds strong trust and loyalty. At Disney, Judson always made himself available to help any Cast Member who came to him, despite his very demanding schedule. He taught leadership, through a fascinating Leadership

---

[16]   Bible, 1 Corinthians 10:12–13

Jazz seminar. He was a major cheerleader for the team, and fought hard to get the resources and rewards necessary to build a world-class culture. He was very focused on business success, but when that success occurred, he gave the credit to his team rather than highlighting himself. He did not fall prey to the pride derailers, and succeeded in life and leadership through humility and service. He has a fruitful legacy in leaders who follow his example and impact the lives of thousands.

Is this the type of leader and person you would like to become? Recognizing the pride derailers and taking steps to foster humility using many of the ideas in this book will promote a lifetime of humble success.

Action Points

- ▸ Recognize that humility is a key requirement for long-term success.
- ▸ Understand your "pride derailers" and take steps to prevent your misperceptions and temptations from destroying you.
- ▸ Ask a good friend to help you know when your pride is harmful to you and others, and remedy the situation.
- ▸ Look for and follow role models of humble success.

Payoff

Continued success, exceptional performance, a lasting legacy.

52. Who Are You? What Do You Want?

*Everything that is really great and inspiring is created
by the individual who can labor in freedom.*
— ALBERT EINSTEIN

*In the truest sense, freedom cannot be
bestowed; it must be achieved.*
— FRANKLIN D. ROOSEVELT

*But whoever looks intently into the perfect law that gives
freedom, and continues in it—not forgetting what they have
heard, but doing it—they will be blessed in what they do.*
— BIBLE, JAMES 1:25

*Christ has set us free to live a free life. So take your stand.
Never again let anyone put a harness of slavery on you.*
— BIBLE, GALATIANS 6:1

I have participated in many facilitated worksessions during my
twenty-plus years in the corporate world. These usually start
with everyone going around the room and introducing him
or herself. At one of those sessions, the facilitator asked us to
answer two questions that profoundly changed the dynamic
of our group: "Who are you?" and "What do you want?" The
facilitator suggested that we answer these questions at a deeper
level than just stating our name and a trite answer like, "I want
the day to be successful." Although all of us in the session had
worked closely together for many years, the answers that we

heard that day gave us a new appreciation of each other as we shared our identities and desires.

How would you answer those two questions? Who are you? What do you want? Over the years as I have pondered the second question, my answer has turned to "freedom."[17]

This freedom is evidenced in four specific areas. The first freedom is physical, defined as a healthy body without limitations. I want to have energy and strength; the ability to run, swim, play, think and create; and, experience life without physical hindrance. This vision of physical freedom motivates me to do the efforts described in Chapter 1, especially when I'm challenged to exercise or eat well. While I can't control the possibility of an accident or serious illness that might cause me to become impaired, I can control and create a routine that promotes healthful longevity and physical freedom.

The second freedom is financial. I want to live without debt, and with adequate financial resources to support my family in a reasonable lifestyle. I want to be generous, and able to give to needs that I see around me. I want appropriate insurance so that I can retain financial stability in the circumstance of a calamitous event. I don't want to have to worry about the ups and downs of the stock market, or have my moods dictated by my portfolio. Chapter 2 specifically deals with money, but there are many ideas in the other chapters that can help you achieve financial freedom.

The third freedom is relational. I want to be on good terms with people, in accordance with the wisdom of the Apostle Paul:

---

[17]   I am particularly indebted to my pastor, David Loveless, who has spoken several times on this topic. Much of this section can be attributed to his wisdom in this area.

"If it is possible, as far as it depends on you, live at peace with everyone."[18] If I have wronged someone, I want their forgiveness and, if someone has wronged me, I want to forgive. Far too many people go to their grave being out of relationship with others, and this is especially tragic if it is a spouse or child. Freedom often requires taking responsibility and saying you are sorry.

It also means being proactive and ensuring those whom you love know it. I listened to a message by a Scottish pastor, Alistair Begg. He said Americans are far too casual about "hellos" and "goodbyes." We often don't notice or remark when someone arrives or leaves. Other cultures make it a point to greet someone warmly and say a thoughtful farewell when someone departs. He referenced spouses and parents that he had consoled after the unexpected death of a loved one who told him they never got to say goodbye or "I love you." After hearing his words, I made it a habit to always tell my family members that I loved them any time we separated, even to make a short trip to the store. This gives me the relational freedom to know that, if one of us were to die, the last words we shared were "I love you." After my mother died following our final trip to see her, it gave me great peace to know those were the last words she heard from me. You are relationally free when you live without regrets concerning people.

The fourth freedom is spiritual. I want to know where I am going after I die and whether I will be reunited with loved ones who died before me. I want to know that I had a purpose for being on the earth. I want to know that I will ultimately understand how the universe was created, why there is evil and suffering, why man was created in the first place, and the

---

[18] Bible, Romans 12:18

answers to other "big" questions. While some may find this spiritual freedom in Judaism, Islam, Buddhism or another belief system, my spiritual freedom comes from being a follower of Jesus Christ. In accepting Christ as my Lord and Savior, I have received peace on this earth and assurance of what comes after death. Knowing how the game ends (and that I win) frees me to meet daily challenges, and "shoots adrenaline into my soul."[19]

Being free in these four ways goes beyond traditional measures of success, and reaches the definition of success surpassing beyond measure.

 ## Action Points

- If you were asked, "Who are you?" and "What do you want?" how would you answer?
- Are you "free"? If not, what binds you and how can you release yourself?
- Think about your hellos and goodbyes. Would you do them differently if you knew you or the other person might not see each other again?

 ## Payoff

Direction, purpose, a life without regrets, freedom.

---

[19] Bible, Hebrews 12:3, Message translation

Conclusion

M Y GOAL IN WRITING *The **Surpassing!** Life* was to help you improve your life and leadership. After sharing some of the ideas in my weekly newsletters, I've received testimonies of the transformative power and positive behaviors readers have experienced as they have put the ideas into action. I hope you have a similar story, and would like to hear from you.

Thanks for reading this, and I hope you now go out and excel beyond measure!

Bring *The Surpassing! Life* to You!
Book Brad Rex For Your Next
Speaking Engagement

Based on his unique life experiences, Brad Rex provides outstanding messages with emotional and intellectual content. Unlike some speakers that provide inspiration but no "meat," Brad shares inspirational stories *and* practical ideas for immediate implementation. Book him today to achieve personal and corporate excellence.

Most Popular Speaker. Inspiring. Practical. Powerful. Engaging.
I oversee the booking of over 100 speaker engagements annually, and Brad is one of our most popular speakers. Business leaders want his inspiring stories and practical ideas from leading at high levels in Disney and Hilton. I highly recommend Brad for any organization seeking powerful, engaging messages that challenge leaders to achieve their highest potential.
—Steven French, President, Lifework Leadership,
www.lifeworkleadership.org

On Target Message. Informative.
Articulate. Humor and Humility.
Brad Rex exceeded our expectations when he spoke to an auditorium full of leaders at our annual community business luncheon. *Feedback from the audience was enthusiastic, positive and supportive. Brad's message was on target for our audience, informative and articulate, and it was delivered with appropriate amounts of humor and humility.* In considering how well a speaker meets our needs, we often consider the question "would we have them back again?". In Brad's case, that answer is a resounding "YES."
—Brad Williams, EVP and Treasurer, CFO,
Simpson University, www.simpsonu.edu

A Favorite Among Elite Speakers. Engaging. Compelling. A Memorable Experience.

Brad is an excellent communicator, and was rated on our survey as one of the favorites among an elite group of speakers and trainers. Brad's engaging style and compelling content made for a memorable experience for all who participated in The Leadership Fellows Program. *The true evidence of his leadership is that many followed his advice and changed their strategies as a result of his insights.*

—Dee Ann Boyd, Director of Leadership Performance
The NYC Leadership Center, www.nycleadership.com

Whether the topic is Leadership, Customer Service, Diversity, Humility or Generosity, Brad motivates, challenges, inspires and humors his audience, while providing practical steps to achieve personal and corporate excellence.

Book Brad Today and Make Your Event A Memorable Success! Go To:

www.bradrexgroup.com

13006379R00122

Made in the USA
Charleston, SC
11 June 2012